FROM
Colic
TO
Collage

CHUCKLING YOUR WAY
THROUGH PARENTHOOD

LINDA FITERMAN

ISBN 1-880654-05-9 (hardcover)
ISBN 1-880654-04-0 (paper trade)

Library of Congress Catalogue Card No. 93-87774.

Interior illustrations by Bill Stein.

Recognition

In recognition of its leadership in helping children succeed for life, the author and the publisher will donate a portion of the proceeds of sale of this book to the United Way of Minneapolis Area.

Dedication

To my incredible husband, Mike, who never once in twenty-two years of parenting together referred to me as a "non-working" mother. And to my children, Jack, Ann and Debra, who in their grandparents' opinion are the most beautiful, talented and intelligent kids on the planet. I tend to agree wholeheartedly.

Foreword

When I became pregnant with my first child twenty-one years ago I was determined to read every textbook, handbook, magazine and newspaper article ever printed on the subjects of pregnancy, birth and child rearing. It didn't take a rocket scientist to soon discover that this feat was not only an impossibility but completely unnecessary. Impossible because there are virtually millions of so-called "experts" on the subject. Unnecessary because none of these millions of experts has the guts to tell it like it really is. This book is a no holds barred rendition of what to expect during those nine fun filled water retentive months and the decades of hilarity after that new little critter invades the family. Who am I to write such a book, you ask? From what university did I get my doctoral degree on this subject? These are fair questions so I'll respond in the most professional and truthful way I know. I've been pregnant for twenty-seven months of my life. During these months collectively I have gained a total of 135 pounds and lost 90 of them. Other than Shamu the killer whale at Sea World, who better than myself to glorify the beauty of gestation? My three children range in ages from thirteen to twenty-two. Over the course of those years I have spent more time in pediatric offices than Donald Trump has spent in Marla Maples' bedroom. I have been a room mother for seventeen consecutive years, packed over ten thousand bag lunches and driven more miles in one day than Mario Andretti covers in a year. If you can relate to a woman who feels that sitting on a metal chair for two and a half hours listening to a first and second grade band concert in a school gymnasium is proper punishment for your average serial killer, then this is the book for you. It won't always be pretty but I'll tell you the real facts of life that even your own mother kept from you.

Contents

Diagnosing The Pregnancy

Discovering you are pregnant can occur in several ways. If it happens to an actress on a soap opera, nine times out of ten she is unmarried, hasn't a clue as to which of her twelve recent "suitors" might be the father, and is most likely to hear the news of her delicate condition just prior to her murder conviction in a small town named Elmdale. Home pregnancy tests have yet to be discovered in soapland leaving our heroine no alternative but to diagnose her pregnancy the old fashioned way by going to the doctor. Daytime television doctors are a breed of their own. They can perform a heart transplant in fifty-two minutes, do neurosurgery between Dreft and Tidybowl commercials and cure African sleeping sickness during their coffee break. But diagnose a women's pregnancy after four missed periods? Three weeks minimum. "I'll call you as soon as the lab results are in, Ericka." This lab no doubt is in the jungles of Brazil and arrives on the back of a lame burro. So poor Ericka waits and waits to find out and the viewer waits and waits to find out. By the time her pregnancy is finally confirmed she's already dilated five centimeters and is severely iron deficient.

"This home pregnancy kit? Oh, this isn't for me!!"

Fortunately things move a bit quicker in real life and women can now learn within minutes whether or not they are indeed in a "motherly" way. Home pregnancy tests are available at all local pharmacies. For many women, however, purchasing the kit is the hardest part of using one. Not unlike the fourteen year old boy who hides a pack of condoms in his shopping cart underneath the cough drops and spearmint gum, she discreetly camouflages the pregnancy test under other purchases like nail polish and corn pads. If she knows the druggist she might feel a need to explain that she is purchasing the kit for her Catholic cleaning lady's daughter-in-law from a first marriage. She hasn't quite figured out why this activity is shrouded in such mystery; she just knows it is.

The results of a home pregnancy test are calculated with amazing speed. While Ericka in television land is sweating it out day after day, you have already gained ten pounds and picked out the nursery furniture.

There are other giveaway hints that you may now have a new "tenant" aboard. When your twenty-four hour bout with the morning "stomach flu" goes into its fifth week and amazingly no other family member has caught it, it's time to reassess your ailment. If you drop a Q-tip on your chest and it takes you four minutes to regain consciousness from "minor" breast tenderness, your body might be sending you another clue.

Whichever way your pregnancy is detected, ladies, hold on to your seats. The nine month journey you are about to take is chock full of adventure.

The Truth, the Whole Truth and Nothing But the Truth About Your Pregnancy

Now that your pregnancy has been confirmed I'm sorry to have to be the one to tell you that neither your body nor your emotions will ever again bear any resemblance to the pre-pregnant you. First, your body. The medical "experts" will tell you that ideally you should gain no more than twenty-five to thirty pounds during the next forty weeks. It is vital that you understand that the key word in this statement is "ideally." Apparently my doctor was not aware of a special ability of mine. You see, on any given non-holiday weekend I can easily gain four to six pounds simply by dining out at favorite restaurants. This is a non-pregnancy skill I have mastered over the years with regularity. Math not being my strongest subject, I was still able to calculate that if I continued at the same weekend pace I would reach my pregnancy weight goal at about seven weeks gestation. Multiplying at this rate, at the end of nine months I would have put on approximately 210 pounds, give or take an ounce. I realized that I had two choices. I could drastically change my eating habits or change doctors. Reluctantly I decided to go the first route and cut back my caloric intake to a mere four thousand calories a day.

Fortunately for me I am blessed with a husband who thinks all pregnant women are beautiful. In his words, "they positively glow" with beauty. Well, if one's girth has any bearing on the amount of glowing they project, let's just say that by the end of the seventh month I could have lit up Canada. I came from the old school of thought that says a lady in waiting should eat for two. I, however, ate enough for two average size circus elephants. My feet were slowly becoming the eighth wonder of the world. Paper towel manufacturers would have killed to have a product that would retain as much water as my ankles did those last few weeks. Shoe straps disappeared into mounds of flesh and the imprint from the buckle would be apparent for hours after removing the shoe. My rings wouldn't budge over swollen knuckles and extra body parts like chins and hanging skin flaps appeared virtually overnight. My husband, bless his little heart, still maintained that I looked like royalty. I stood before him in my ninth month and asked him if he still thought I looked like a queen. "Absolutely", he lovingly answered. "The Queen Mary." By then I had lost my once keen sense of humor. He never joked again.

The "experts" also speak of emotional ups and downs which might occur during those magical nine months. Ups and downs? Another poor choice of words I would suggest. "Hormonal havoc" is perhaps a better definition when suddenly out of nowhere a woman in her second trimester is convinced that the trashman is making sexual advances towards her. When a woman's husband informs her of an upcoming night of poker with the boys, is she merely having a bad hair day when she hires a noted mafia hit man to break up the game? I wouldn't think so. There are pregnancy hormones at play here that even Masters and Johnson wouldn't attempt to tame. The best thing to do is accept them as a normal part of the program and pray that during those forty weeks you are able to stay out of all state correctional institutions.

My husband thought I was so beautiful in my ninth month of pregnancy. He said I looked like a queen!

What the Childbirth Classes Tell You

The 1970's brought a bold new concept into the business of pregnancy and birth. Practically overnight fathers were booted out of the waiting rooms on maternity floors and into the battlefields of the labor and delivery rooms with their partners. We always knew that the male member of this relationship was at the scene of the crime when conception took place. But where were these same fellas when it was curtain time some 40 weeks later? In our parents' days Mr. Macho was pacing the hospital corridors and putting in orders for Cuban cigars at the local tobacco store. Well, the party's over, boys. You helped the little lady get into this ball game, you stay for the whole nine innings.

And so the happy couple signs up for six weeks of childbirth classes. At each session the two hour format is broken up into four 30 minute intervals. The first half hour usually consists of a group discussion where all the women compare annoying little symptoms with each other such as six day heartburn attacks, the inability to clip one's toenails, the inability to see one's toenails and alien brown lines stretching from the navel to the bikini area.

9

During the second half hour the woman lies down on floor mats with pillows tucked under her knees. Her partner who is now officially known as "coach" sits beside her and together they learn to breathe and count. Call me silly but I was always brought up to believe that breathing was one of those involuntary skills that most human beings mastered the moment the doctor's hand smacked our bottoms at birth. Is this instructor implying that I've been doing it wrong all these years? And how about this counting business? Why can't expectant fathers just boil water and rip up clean sheets like they did on "Bonanza" and "Little House On the Prairie?" I know my husband can count. He knows he can count. Is it really necessary that he review these basic skills during this critical time in our lives? So I breathed and he counted. I panted and he counted. If breathing and counting make for a healthy baby who was I to question it?

During the third half hour we watched a movie on childbirth. The actress in the film looked pretty darn good, I thought. Eyeliner still in place, not a bead of sweat rolling down her Clinique-covered cheekbones and a hint of a Mona Lisa smile on her pursed lips as she breathed and panted to the rhythm of her husband's melodic counting. With about the same force it takes me to clear my throat in the morning, she expelled a perfectly formed wailing newborn, peered into her physician's eyes with gratitude, and, with a sigh, lapsed into a peaceful slumber holding her new son in her loving arms. I looked at the other couples in the room as they watched the movies. The women were all crying. The husbands were counting. It was such a beautiful movie that it could have won an Oscar at the Academy Awards. What none of us unsuspecting fools realized then, however, was that it would have won the Oscar for best performance by an actress in a science fiction presentation.

The final thirty minutes of the class was my favorite time by far. Our group was taken up to the hospital nursery where we could view this year's models through a glass partition. Babies in various lengths, head circumferences, and leaking body parts peered at the gawking strangers with huge bellies. All of the mothers-to-be smiled and cooed at these amazing little people. Our husbands counted.

And so it went for six consecutive weeks. Talking, breathing, counting, and viewing. We were all prepared by the "experts" for the main event. So we thought.

What the Childbirth Classes Didn't Tell You

I hardly even know where to begin on this one. Do you remember that breathing stuff they taught you in class? Do you recall the counting exercise you rehearsed so diligently day after day? Will you ever forget the adoration you felt for your "coach" as you practiced together in anticipation of the thrilling adventure in store for you both? The answers to these questions are "no," "give me a break," and "what coach?" Except in the most extreme cases, all recollections and memories of any birth preparation course have immediately left you upon the first twinge of labor.

First, the truth about this breathing business. The childbirth class neglected to teach you a critical skill. How to swear, breathe and count all at the same time. Believe me when I tell you it is an impossibility to do all three simultaneously. Not in any classroom or pregnancy textbook does it explain how to breathe while calling your nurse, doctor and significant other a son of a b. I think you get the point. You see even the most genteel lady, one who was educated in an English finishing school, is transformed into the Wicked Witch of the West in the hospital labor room. Women who sing in the church choir

Counting is not the first activity that comes into the mind of a woman in hard labor. Killing or permanently maiming someone beyond recognition is a bit more accurate.

are barking vicious obscenities at anyone who even dares hint that perhaps they are not breathing properly. And let me offer another observation of this seething female during labor.

When she feels that a Patriot missile is playing havoc with her insides, counting is not the first activity that comes into mind. Killing or permanently maiming someone beyond recognition is a bit more accurate.

Now let's chat a moment about this "coach" of hers. During the dress rehearsals in the classroom this person, most often the future dad, starred as supporting actor. He talked softly to her, wiped her brow, and offered her ice chips to soothe her parched lips. All this to help make labor and delivery a much more pleasant experience. Very noble and fine ideas on paper. However, this is not dress rehearsal. It's opening night, buddy, and you can talk, soothe and ice chip her to death, but don't expect her to gaze back at you with loving eyes in gratitude. When she is having contractions every minute that last 56 seconds and is only dilated to three centimeters she ain't gonna be Mother Teresa. To put it even more bluntly, it won't matter to her if you or Attila the Hun is with her. Just get this thing over with, now. One thing that she will vow, however, somewhere between 2 and 10 centimeters, is that never will this child ever have a sibling. On occasion she may become hostile to the gentleman who got her into this situation. One woman threatened to take her husband to court for concealing a lethal weapon in his boxer shorts. Fortunately for him and the future of the human race, once all the shouting is over and that new little person is lying in her arms, most memories of the past 12 or more hours slowly fade into a dark corner of her brain not to reappear again until another bundle of joy is on its way. Mother nature works in strange ways.

Revealing the Mystery of The Hospital Suitcase

Throughout the history of mankind there are certain material objects which play a dramatic role in life. Since the birth of Christianity men have given their very lives in search for the Holy Grail. Scholars through the years have studied the mysteries of the Dead Sea Scrolls and the wonders of the Egyptian pyramids have kept archeologists at work for centuries. Ranking right up there in importance with the Bill of Rights of the Constitution and the invention of the wheel is the phenomenon of the infamous hospital suitcase. After three children, however, I have to confess I haven't a clue as to what the purpose of this suitcase is. With clockwork accuracy, on the first day of a woman's ninth month of pregnancy she decides it is time to pack for the hospital. She gets out the trusty manual given to her at childbirth classes and proceeds to read the list of items necessary to bring to the hospital when the big day arrives:

1. Toothbrush and toothpaste
2. Nightgowns, bathrobe and slippers
3. Lollipops

4. Tennis balls
5. A deck of playing cards
6. Stationery and writing pens
7. A camera and film
8. Outfits for mother and baby to wear going home

Looking at this list for the first time immediately raises a few questions. For example, why the tennis balls? Dozens of your friends and relatives have given birth. Do you recall even one of them ever suggesting, "Tennis anyone?" between labor contractions? Obviously not. So why the tennis balls, you ask once again. According to childbirth experts, as well as Martina Navratilova and Jimmy Connors, women who are experiencing the joy of back labor, along with everything else, will find some brief relief when their backs are gently massaged with tennis balls. Personally speaking, I don't know if this works or not. I would suggest packing the balls anyway so they can be hurled at any medical person who cheerfully asks you during your 18 hour labor, "How are we feeling, Dearie?"

Another rather questionable item on the "what to pack for the hospital" list is the deck of playing cards. As you were told in childbirth class, "Labor is often a long and tedious process. Some couples find that playing cards will help pass the time." I often wonder which hallucinatory drug the deranged pervert who made this suggestion was using? Just ask any woman who has been admitted to the hospital to give birth what her first request was. I would be willing to stake my life that it was rarely for a friendly game of gin rummy.

The stationery and pen? Well, it was a fine suggestion back in prehistoric times when a woman could stay in the hospital for more than a two day stretch. But who exactly is she going to write to anyway? By the time all her friends and family hear the big news, she's already been evicted from the hospital and a new tenant is in her room.

Examining the list further we see the items of camera and film. Now this is just fine and dandy as long as it is made perfectly clear to the photographer, whoever he or she might be, that under no circumstance are you, the mother, ever to be the subject of a photograph while in the process of labor and delivery. Strictly speaking this is such a mandatory requirement that a simple oral promise will not suffice but rather a notarized legal document will be necessary. Believe me when I tell you that when you are sweating, panting, and cursing you will not feel like either Christie Brinkley, Cheryl Tiegs or any other Super model. So save the camera, still, slide or video, for the kid. Always remember pictures of you will only be useful for blackmail at a later date.

The purpose of the lollipops is a twofold one as I see it. The "experts" tell you to throw a few in your hospital bag to suck on when your lips and mouth get dry during labor. I'm telling you to bring them for a different reason altogether. When your helpful little buddy the coach reminds you for the one thousandth time to breathe to the rhythm of his counting, gently jam one of these suckers, preferably the all day variety, into his annoying little mouth or any other body crevice which you find handy, if you get my drift.

The nightgowns, bathrobe, slippers, and toiletry items are fine to bring but, again, not a necessity. Most new moms find the glamorous hospital gowns just too luxurious to pass up. Also a woman 24 hours postpartum isn't exactly a walking advertisement for a Victoria's Secret negligee. For practical reasons alone the hospital duds work fine. The toothpaste and toothbrush she'll find in her patient admitting kit so those, too, can be left at home.

Finally, a word about the going home outfits for baby and mom. You probably have picked out the most adorable outfit you ever laid eyes upon for junior to go home in. Little embroidered yellow ducks lazily swim on the sleeves and fluffy white clouds adorn the collar and footies. You oohed and ahhed at it over and over again after you brought it home. You folded it oh so gingerly in your bag and smoothed out the wrinkles for nearly five long months. I am going to tell you right now that the odds of your child wearing this outfit home from the hospital are about twelve to one. I would almost guarantee you that someone with major clout in your life like your mother, mother-in-law or oldest sister will march into your hospital room, proudly hand you a gift wrapped package and announce that this is to be the baby's going home outfit. You open it and immediately see that it is a hand knit number that the giver of the gift has been working on for seven and a half months. She also tells you that sending a new baby home in a hand knit sleeper has been a family tradition for ninety-five years. Are you going to be the one to break with tradition only five years short of a century mark? Of course you're not. So you bundle the kid up in the wardrobe from grandma and your duck and cloud dream outfit goes home with the tags still attached.

The final item on the list is an outfit for you. I'm going to put this as gently as I possibly can. You know that maternity pants outfit you wore when you were admitted to the hospital two days ago? Yes, the same one you vowed you would burn the moment you came home from the hospital? This is what you will wear on your journey home. As much as you fantasized about those size eight Calvin Klein jeans, this is all they will remain for at least six months: a fantasy. So just slip into that obscene maternity uniform for your grand hospital exit and pray that no one stops you on the way out and asks, "And when are you due, dear?"

So as you can see, the drama and fuss of the hospital suitcase is highly overrated. When the time comes to leave for the hospital, forget the suitcase and just worry about getting yourself there safely. Mother nature will take care of the rest.

The Truth About Your Hospital Stay

Whern I began to write this book I made a solemn promise to myself not to quote the stories my mother told me about how things "used to be" when she was a new mother. But when talking about hospital stays it really is necessary to look at past trends in order to fully understand how drastically things have changed.

When I was born (after World War II and before hula hoops) new mothers were treated like royalty. An average hospital stay for a natural birth ranged somewhere between ten days and two weeks. On the eighth day postpartum a mom was allowed to sit gingerly on the edge of her bed and dangle her fragile legs for a minute or two. By day ten she had bathroom privileges and finally after half a month she was wheeled carefully out to the family automobile. By the time a new mother left the confines of her hospital room, every incision had healed and junior was practically ready for nursery school.

That was four decades ago. Well, welcome to the 90's where the last time a new mother stayed in the hospital longer than a week she made front page news in the National Enquirer. The average hospital stay for an uncomplicated labor and delivery

By the time the new mother is wheeled into her own room, she is greeted by a nurse's aide to go over her discharge papers.

is currently two days. It is also necessary to understand that in most hospitals a day begins and ends at 12:00 midnight. Therefore if a woman enters the hospital at 6:00 P.M. and delivers at 12:05 A.M. she has already used up one of her days before the kid gives his first scream. By the time the new mother is wheeled into her own room, she is greeted by a nurse's aide to go over her discharge papers.

Most hospitals today have a program called "rooming in" where the newborn, assuming there are no medical concerns, stays with his mom during the entire hospital stay. When I say entire, I mean as in twenty-four hours a day. Now I loved cuddling up to my new son just as much as the next new mom. I adored feeding him, singing to him and examining his ten precious little fingers and toes. But I had a vicious selfish streak that no one in the hospital was aware of. I simply wanted a few uninterrupted nights of sleep. I knew that the moment I left the hospital with this new family addition, a blissful night's sleep was out of the question for at minimum the next 120 days. Therefore when the perky little nurse inquired if my baby would be "rooming in" for the entire hospital stay (as lengthy as it was) you can just about imagine the disgust in her eyes when I turned down the offer. News of my neglect spread quickly throughout the maternity ward. Medical staff whispered in hushed tones about the woman in 305 who didn't want her kid with her in the room at night. If I had stayed another day I'm convinced that Oprah or Sally Jessy Raphael would have asked me to appear on their shows. By the way, this "baby" is now 22 years old. Except for an occasional outbreak of teenage acne, I saw no damaging affects on his growth or social skills.

During your hospital stay you will probably have the opportunity to attend a bath for baby demonstration. If this is your first child, under no circumstances should you miss this class. Most of the childbirth preparation courses neglect this area altogether. The ones who do touch on it use a well worn Cabbage Patch doll as their bath model. Take it from me. Practicing bathing techniques on a rag doll rather than on a live slippery infant is like preparing for lovemaking with Robert Redford by shaking hands with Woody Allen. There simply is no comparison.

Diapering 101, is another one of those "must attend" classes before you leave the safe confines of the hospital. Actually it would not be a bad idea to invite Grandma or Grandpa along for this little workshop as well. For you see the plumbing on babies hasn't changed since they raised their kids, but the business of diapering has, enormously. The days of diaper pins went out with the Beatles and were replaced with a sturdy and very noisy form of masking tape. Babies are being literally "Ziplocked" all over the world. I know I run the risk of heavy duty lawsuits slapped on me by disposable diaper manufacturers worldwide, but I feel it is my duty to warn you of a slight mis-truth in advertising about this product. It is claimed that the tapes that hold Junior's diaper on are re-usable. In other words if you discover upon examination that your baby is still dry, you may simply re-tape the same diaper shut. I compare this move to opening the oven door half way through a cake's baking time. Trust me when I tell you that just as your cake will fall to the floor in record time, so will Junior's "re-taped" diaper!

The true moment of reckoning comes when you are ready to leave the hospital. Your husband leaves to get the car. An orderly leads the procession down the hospital halls pushing a large cart filled with flowers, candy, stuffed animals, that special suitcase, and infant supplies to see you through the first few days at home. A nurse gets you settled in a wheelchair for the ride to the front door, gently lays your bundled baby in your arms and true realization finally hits you. After all the breathing, counting and swearing this kid is really going home with you.

Cold Hard Facts About Bonding and Baby Blues

Women have been giving birth ever since Adam gave Eve his fraternity pin. Loving her child immediately after setting eyes upon him or her seemed like the natural thing to do. But liking the kid is another story altogether. "Bonding" is the hip term used by experts to describe the intense emotional pull between parent and child. Book after book details the undying devotion a new mom feels towards this little creature she helped create. Hallmark and Hollywood have further instilled this instant love perception with gooey greeting cards and schmaltzy movies complete with forty piece orchestras in mock studio delivery rooms. A woman's life has been fulfilled and never before have such happiness and bliss permeated her very being. Beautiful scenario, right? Beautiful but straight out of la-la land, I'm sorry to say. You see, in reality, the average new parent is so shell-shocked by the abrupt change in life style brought on by this wrinkled damp house guest that he or she wouldn't recognize bliss if it hit them squarely between the eyeballs.

Looking at life as if it were a stage play things might go as follows:

SCENE ONE

After a day at work you and your partner relax with a glass of wine over a quiet dinner. You discuss work, current events and relish heated but always challenging political discussions with each other. You might meet good friends later for a movie followed by dessert and coffee at that wonderful French cafe down by the river. On weekends you and your mate go hiking along rustic trails, run barefoot through lush fields of clover and simply marvel at the wealth nature has to offer.

SCENE TWO

Junior arrives and enters the family unit. Mom and Dad are working hard to bond with the little guy just like it says in the childcare books.

SCENE THREE

After two months of sleep deprivation Mom and Dad are no longer speaking in full sentences. The same two people who once enjoyed a power packed debate on gun control and nuclear freeze are now overwhelmed by vital statistics. How many times did Freddie spit up today? How often did he make ca-ca? What time did he have his bath? How many ounces did he drink at the 4:00 A.M. feeding? They have no recollection of a life prior to Pampers and pacifiers. A romantic outing for them now is going to Wal-Mart on Double Coupon Day. So you see this bonding business isn't as easy as it's cracked up to be.

Lack of sleep is one of the greatest bonding obstacles in life. It's tough enough to love this demanding little intruder when you're awake, let alone when you're half conscious. My husband and I worked out a great system the second week our son came home from the hospital. We agreed that the one who

26

"What baby? I don't hear a baby! Do you hear a baby?"

heard him cry first in the middle of the night would get up to feed him. The first few nights we were both so excited by the little tyke that regardless of which one heard him first, we both fought over who would get to feed him his bottle. When looking back on it I actually recall his sprinting to the nursery in record setting time. By the fifth night the novelty of the little guy had worn thin and now both of us played possum when we heard his first weak whimper of hunger. We did our best to wake the other while pretending to be asleep ourselves. We'd toss, kick, cough and do just about everything short of setting off the smoke alarm to get the other's attention. Finally one of us would relent and go to the battlefield.

Now I would like to share something with you ladies out there who have yet to think of an innovative way to convince the dads to take a night shift feeding. The next time you feed little Herbert or colicky Gloria at 2:00 A.M., snap on the television to the cable shopping network. Order something that you would ordinarily never purchase in a department store. You know, something like ginza knives or the Jack LaLane Juicer. Take my word, you can nag and coerce him to death to take a midnight feeding but nothing works as effectively as a maxed-out Visa bill at the end of the month. If you can prove to him that it is financially dangerous for you to take the graveyard feeding shift, your problems are solved.

When the bonding does finally happen I guarantee you that the glue will last a lifetime.

Sometime during that bonding process a new mom might experience what are commonly known as the baby blues. Until my last child was born thirteen years ago, I was not qualified to speak out on this affliction. My first two pregnancies concluded with happy healthy babies and an equally happy if somewhat exhausted mom.

Number three was different, however. I still came home with the happy and robust baby. I, on the other hand had a slight case of the blues. Actually, it was worse than blue, more like purple. It was the silly little things that set me off crying. Like the Kleenex box being empty when I took my makeup off at night. Like my watch running four minutes slow. I knew I was over the edge when I went to vote in the 1980 presidential election. Election day came one week after my baby was born. After crying for ten minutes in the voting booth a kind blue haired lady from the League of Women Voters tapped me gently on the shoulder and asked if she could be of help. I completely lost it and sobbed that I simply didn't know whom to vote for. She said it probably wouldn't be the deciding vote in the electoral system. She tried but she simply didn't understand. How could she when I didn't get it myself?

I came out of the "baby purples" gradually within a couple of weeks. The deciding factor in my total recovery I attribute to my mother. Perceptive as she was she thought the answer to my problems might be a day away from the baby. I had more like a month in mind, but I agreed. I hired a babysitter and together with my mom and sister spent the afternoon having lunch out and going to a movie. Sounds great, right? Except the movie we saw was "The Elephant Man." Now anyone who has ever seen this movie can attest to the fact that it was probably the most depressing and melancholy 120 minutes ever produced in the history of film making. But miracles of miracles, it was exactly what I needed to pull myself together. I mean this guy's life was so dismal that I realized what a great thing I had going for myself. I've said it before, but it bears repeating. Nature works in mysterious ways.

Losing the Pregnancy Weight

How much weight your doctor "allows" you to gain during your pregnancy depends, of course, on each individual case. I never claimed to be an expert in all areas of gestation and child rearing; however on the subject of weight gain, or as I more commonly call it "tonnage," I am the grand master.

I have been pregnant and fortunate enough to have given birth to three healthy full term babies. I learned early on in my first pregnancy that there are two critical rules to follow regarding weight management and your monthly doctor visit. First, it is imperative to go to the appointment on an empty stomach. Obviously this means that never if at all possible do you schedule an afternoon checkup. You will need all the help you can get on that day to keep that scale's needle from creeping up any higher than necessary. After the appointment by all means consume everything in sight, including dessert. After all you won't be checking in with the warden for another three to four weeks. The other basic rule to insure the least possible weight gain is to choose your appointment wardrobe very carefully. I don't care if it's fifty below zero with a windchill of double that

amount outside, never wear a heavy sweater or sweat pants to the doctor's office. The first place they put you before you can even get both water packed feet in the door is on the scale. Why would you want to load yourself down with heavy garments when shorts and a tank top barely weigh half a pound?

So what if it's a bit drafty and you're the recipient of a few strange looks in the waiting room. Trust me when I assure you it's worth it for the weigh in ceremony.

During my first pregnancy I gained a modest 28 pounds and delivered a seven and a half pound baby boy. I was nearly textbook perfect in my weight gain, obeying doctor's orders to stay within a 25-30 pound range. When I left the hospital I had a mere eight pounds to lose; an amount barely worth talking about. During my second pregnancy two years later I was advised to keep my weight gain within this same 25-30 pound span. I wasn't quite as successful this time around, gaining a rather respectable forty-two pounds. When my baby girl tipped the scales at a petite 6 pounds, 11 ounces, I knew that regaining my pre-pregnant figure would take a bit longer that the first go around.

> WARNING: The following paragraph contains graphic material which may be unsuitable for the weak of heart or for any woman currently in any trimester of gestation.

My third pregnancy began harmlessly enough. I had changed gynecologists after my first two children were born so I thought it was only fair to brief him on my two previous nine month adventures. As I told him about my twenty-eight pound weight gain he nodded and smiled approvingly. When he learned of my forty-two pound pregnancy he shook his head, clicked his tongue three times and announced professionally, "I will not allow you to do this again." He was totally right. I didn't gain forty-two pounds. I put on a whopping sixty-five big ones!

You're probably wondering about now, among other things, how my new doctor reacted to this? What did he do? What did he say? Let me put it to you this way. Here was a man about five foot four weighing in at approximately 140 pounds minus his stethoscope. I, in comparison, was a woman five foot seven resembling your average sumo wrestler. What was he supposed to say to me? He's a bright guy. He's keenly aware of the fact that if he assaulted me with any snide weight gain remarks I could literally kill him with the flick of one swollen index finger.

I was an amazing sight, those final two months. Friends and relatives began to make bets on the weight of this child. Ex-friends and relatives made bets on my weight as well. Twelve years ago ultra sound was only done on pregnancies in trouble which mine thankfully was not. So because of my tremendous girth people suspected an impending multiple birth. Although my doctor claimed he only detected one heart beat, surely with my mounds and mounds of spare flesh, an extra kid or two could easily hide out for forty unsuspecting weeks.

When the big day arrived and I was wheeled into the delivery room I was convinced that either this child would go straight from the hospital nursery into kindergarten, or I would be the latest entry in the Guinness Book of World Records under the category of largest newborn litters. Fortunately it was a quick delivery. I had gained so much weight that even the birth canal was crowded and anxious for a hasty evacuation. After only a 45 minute wait the delivery was over. Dying from curiosity I screamed, "How many and how much do they weigh?" The obstetrician, nurses, and aides all hovered around as if they were about to witness an historical moment. "One baby girl," the doctor announced. Almost afraid to hear the answer to the next question I hesitantly asked what her weight was. "Seven pounds, two ounces," was the reply. So there I was on the delivery table with this wrinkled, bald newest family member in my arms and I began to do some quick math calculations in my head. The kid weighed seven

pounds, two ounces, the placenta maybe another two or three pounds. I factored in an additional three pounds of amniotic fluid and two for uterus growth. Without the aid of a calculator, I quickly determined that I had fifty-one pounds unaccounted for. I asked the doctor to check one more time just to make sure he didn't forget someone up there. He assured me that I was indeed a single room apartment with only one tenant. And so three days later I left the hospital with my darling new daughter and more pounds to lose than my total second pregnancy weight gain. I guess I should have skipped the dessert after those post doctor visit lunches.

What's in a Name?

Choosing a name for your baby can be as simple or as complicated as you want it to be. If you come from a family that automatically tacks on the title of "Jr." to the first born male, the decision is already made for you. But if you're the kind who insists that each child deserves his or her own identity, the Jr. system of naming is an unacceptable option.

There are essentially four different methods which new parents use when deciding on a name for their child. The first way is the "Keeping it Simple" method of baby naming. These parents believe that life is hard enough without having a name that people can't either pronounce or spell. Chances are that they had extremely difficult names themselves when growing up. Because they grew so tired of always correcting teachers, employers and co-workers they made a vow to themselves that when they had to name their own kids, it would be virtually impossible for anyone to flub it up. That is where all the Johns, Jims and Marys of the world come from. I once heard of a woman, Martha, who had four sons all named Henry. She said she did this to make her life easier. When she called "Henry, time for dinner" all four boys sat down. When she yelled up-stairs, "Henry, time for bed," she knew that all four would soon be down for the night. One day a friend asked Martha, "What happens when you only want to talk to one son?" Without a moment's hesitation Martha answered, "Then I call them by their last name."

The second method parents might choose when selecting a name for their baby is naming them after a deceased relative. This is a fine idea as long as every piece of information about that relative you intend to honor is known. Nothing could be worse than naming your newborn after sainted cousin Tilly only to find out two years later that good ole Tilly had a little family business on the side which hired out "Ladies of the Evening" to please travelling salesmen passing in the night. Discovering that cousin Tilly was indeed Madame Tilly could be unsettling to say the least. Once you do all your homework and can be assured that your baby's namesake is "kosher" in every respect, then go ahead and pass on the name for the next generation to enjoy.

The third method of baby name selection usually stems from the combined culture of the two parents. When Timothy O'Leary and Kelly McDougal marry and have a baby three years later no one will be surprised when the baby is christened Patrick O'Leary. However our world is a rich blending of many nationalities and a virtual melting pot of countless cultures. What is more likely to happen is that beautiful Indira Ma-hatma from Bangladesh will meet Sven Carlson from Norway one day at a United Nations youth rally in Cleveland. They'll fall in love, tie the knot and give birth to a bouncing baby boy named Mohammed Carlson. Try going through life with a name like that. I also heard a rather amusing tale some time ago about an Native American woman who married a gentle-man of the Jewish faith. Wanting to observe the traditions of both cultures they named their darling baby girl Whitefish.

The fourth and final way couples come to choose their baby's name is the most ingenious of all. They decide to name the kid after the place in which he or she was conceived. Now that works just find in some situations as in the case of baby Virginia who might have gotten her start in the state of the same name. Babies with more exotic names such as Madison, Cheyenne or Hartford will probably be a bit curious when they get older as to the origin of their rather unconventional names. Parents who choose this method of naming better be prepared to come up with some pretty straight answers to some pretty hairy questions. Obviously this method does not work in every situation. If it did the world would be swarming with kids named Chevy, Nissan and Toyota. The most unusual story I have ever heard about naming a baby has to be the one about the couple who were in a weekly bowling league together. One night they "celebrated" their team's victory in a rather torrid way behind the men's locker room. Nine months later they were the proud parents of a nine pound two ounce baby boy. They named him Brunswick.

Buying the Basics

Simple rules of logic would lead you to believe that small things need small spaces in which to exist. For example, if you bought only one goldfish, you would purchase a comfortable one quart bowl for him to swim about in. Keeping with the marine life theme, if you chose instead to house twenty or thirty finned friends, a twenty or thirty gallon aquarium would be the appropriate choice. When examining the requirements of one standard size infant, however, this theory of "small for small" doesn't even begin to apply.

An average baby, wet or dry, will tip the scales anywhere between five and ten pounds, give or take a few ounces. Even in the most extreme cases where the tiniest peanuts might weigh in at two or three pounds or the heavyweights will challenge the record books at twelve or more pounds, every new baby could certainly be carried around effortlessly in the crook of an adult's arm. One would assume that anything which takes up such a minute amount of space on earth would logically not require a great expanse of area in order to exist. Here is where the theory goes radically haywire.

Sometime during your pregnancy you decide it's time to

The best things in life might be free, but the basics don't come cheap.

shop for your future child's "basics." Let's examine this word "basics" for a moment. Never in the history of the English language has there been such confusion over the definition of one word. What does it mean? You as a soon-to-be parent are totally stumped by its implication. The dictionary defines basics as those which are essential in life. By your interpretation that translates into the food, clothing, and shelter categories. So keeping those three things in mind you head out to the local shopping mall.

The food part you realize has to wait until junior is actually around and direct communication begins between you and pediatric headquarters. You must however buy the paraphernalia it will take to feed the little tyke. So you begin by taking inventory of the baby bottle department. There are white ones, florescent, clear, flowered, paisley, Disney-stamped and checkered bottles. Do you get the standard shaped or the ones with the loop-like formation so junior can hold it himself? And what about the ones with the plastic bags inside? Are they biodegradable? Will you have to worry about the plastic exploding half way through a feeding? What kind of feeding dish do you decide on? Do you buy the electric ones that heat the food in ninety seconds or do you worry that someone will trip over the cord and break a body part they really can't do without? Maybe you should go the old fashioned route and buy the food warming dish that heats up in ten minutes while it rests in an inner container of hot water. But ten minutes can be an eternity when junior is screaming for breakfast and you're already running late for work. Perhaps it would be best to forego the warming dish altogether and rely on your trusty microwave to heat the meals. But then again what was that article you just read at the dentist's office and which claimed a link between microwaves and sterility? You want to be a grandmother one day, don't you? What if the kid eats strained peaches heated in the microwave and finds out in twenty-five years he's impotent? Are you prepared to live with that for the rest of your life?

Next, you stroll over to assess the high chairs. The early American ones with the wooden trays would match the decor of the kitchen but you heard somewhere that it was a constant struggle getting peanut butter out of the wooden nuts and bolts which held the thing together. That cute yellow one with the Little Mermaid design was adorable but when your child number two or three uses it five to ten years down the road will the Little Mermaid be in some Disneyland nursing home for outdated animated characters? Would having the Little Mermaid on his tray be dangerous for your son's self-esteem? Better stick to Mickey or Minnie. They'll be around forever.

Selecting your baby's crib falls under the shelter portion of the list of basics. The choices offered to you are staggering. Do you want light or dark wood? Does the paint on this crib chip off when the teething months begin? Is this one with the curvy spindles too feminine in case you have a boy? On the other hand if your baby turns out to be a girl are we taking the risk of labeling her as "delicate" or too soft to compete in a male-biased world? What if she can't get the job of district attorney thirty years down the road because somehow those curvy spindles on her crib sent out negative subliminal messages?

How many sets of sheets do you buy? What's today's theory on giving the kid a pillow? What's a bumper pad? Isn't that something covered under your car warrantee? Ok, you've made the final decision on which crib to buy. Just as the salesman is computing the sales tax he asks you, "And what will baby be sleeping in during the daytime?" Excuse me. What did this guy just say? You just spent $769.95 on the crib. For that kind of money you sort of figured the kid would sleep in it around the clock for at least three years and he's mumbling something about the daytime? "Well you know, studies have shown that a newborn does far better when he can be within earshot and eye range of his adult caregiver," Mr. Salesman continues. Now this situation seems rather ludicrous when you really think about it. Here's a guy who works for minimum wage in the city's largest discount store and you listen to him as if he's a child psychologist from the Mayo Clinic. So you take Dr. Wal-Mart's advice and add a $129.98 portable bassinet to your quickly expanding bill.

Moving to the clothing department you sift through the racks of one piece nighties and pajamas with feet. If you are a first time parent I can almost guarantee that you will buy too many small sizes and not nearly enough larger ones. Please take heed. Never buy any garment that says 0-10 pounds in the label. Your baby will outgrow this piece of clothing on the ride home from the hospital. Even if your little guy is a mere 5½ pounds, he will need the next size sleeper before you purchase your second box of Dreft. If you don't take my word on this one, be prepared to have to go on another shopping excursion much sooner than you expected. You will however, have a lovely collection of Cabbage Patch and Barbie Doll clothes when your child gets older. Don't forget to purchase under-shirts for your baby. He won't need them but the baby's grand-mother won't give you a day of peace until her grandchild has them for those "chilly" 90 degree August nights. Booties are cute but a complete waste. The current record for a baby keep-ing both booties on without losing one is 45 minutes. Also it helps to remember when clothes shopping for your soon-to-be family member that friends and relatives are your best source for gifts of cute but totally impractical babywear. Save the frilly stuff, bow ties and suspenders for the baby showers and hospi-tal visits. Otherwise you'll have your hands full returning the duplicates.

So now you're saying to yourself, alright I covered the "ba-sics" of food, shelter and clothing. That's about it, right? Not so fast. There seem to be a "few" other little items we haven't covered yet, such as the playpen, baby swing, infant seat, car seat (both newborn and toddler variety), Johnny Jump Up (a device that spring loads your kid from any door in the house), umbrella stroller, conventional stroller, walker, potty chair, changing table, and portable bathtub.

In very rare cases (about 99.8%) new parents may find that outfitting their little critter may be beyond their financial abil-ity. They then appeal to friends and relatives who might have unused baby paraphernalia laying around, collecting dust. It's a wonderful option for expectant parents to have as long as they understand two important principles of the "baby-borrowing equipment theory." First, if the cradle, high chair, baby buggy and dresser are all painted a beautiful royal blue and adorned with decals of footballs, baseballs and hockey sticks, you can have absolute assurance that the child you are pregnant with is a girl. I don't care what the ultra-sound or amniocentesis tests say, this kid is definitely of the female variety. Secondly, it is critical to understand that whoever you borrow the crib from will likewise find herself pregnant within two months of the borrowing date. It makes no difference if this woman had her tubes tied ten years ago and her husband is shooting blanks. Once she gets rid of the crib, Mother Nature decides it's time to play an April Fool's stunt big time.

So, if you decide to borrow, the best of luck to you. If you are able to buy everything new, dig out all those savings bonds you might have received as gifts for graduation or your wedding. You'll need to cash in a few of them. For you see the best things in life might be free, but the "basics" don't come cheap.

My Kid's Smarter Than Your Kid

You swore to yourself you would never do it. You made solemn vows that you were above comparing your kid, little Norman, to that little squirt Harold down the block. Every article you ever laid your hands upon in the doctor's office told you that each kid develops at his own speed and in all good time most every tyke will catch up with his peers. Well, I hate to be the fly in the diaper ointment but once again this is a mighty fine theory which rarely if ever happens. Oh the kids will eventually catch up with one another, you understand. But regardless of a new mom or dad's educational level or basic intelligence, there is often an inability to grasp this simple concept. You see, something snaps in a new parent's brain the moment their child takes its first breath of outside air. A flurry of statistics are thrown at them within their baby's first hours of life. "Little Beverly is 7 pounds 8 ounces, Mrs. Brown. She's 19½ inches long with a head circumference of 13½ inches!" What magical numbers these are. Over and over you replay these vital statistics in your head and rattle them off to family members, friends and the cleaning lady who dusts your hospital room. Just when you thought it was safe to call the Superior Infant Modeling Agency, your new roommate is wheeled into your room with some very disturbing revelations. Her little Molly weighs 7 pounds 10 ounces, is 20½ inches long and has a whopping head circumference of 14 inches. Suddenly your kid's statistics pale in comparison and that evil nuisance in life, "K C S" better known as Kid Comparative Syndrome, creeps onto the scene. As much as you try not to succumb to its grip, new parents everywhere suffer under the control of "K C S." Certainly no new mom or dad will ever admit to stooping so low as to having this syndrome but trust me when I assure you that this is a universally experienced shortcoming in life.

Probably one of the most common arenas where Kid Comparative Syndrome happens is when your child walks. Picture the following scene. You and baby Henry are in a play group with other new parents and their toddlers. Without question, Henry is the brightest and most gorgeous child in the group. (This fact was indeed corroborated by both sets of Henry's grandparents when they visited the group the week before.) Henry is eleven months old and has not yet attempted to take a first step, preferring instead his reliable crawl which has proven so effective for his current needs. Enter obnoxious Clifford, that unpleasant nine month old with the flaming red hair and chronic running nose. Clifford (whose grandparents thankfully live out of town) walks up to Henry. Yes, walks upright on two sturdy legs and maniacally rips the toy truck away from your precious Henry's hands. Now what should you as Henry's parent do in this very common situation?

A. Calmly explain to Clifford that if he ever touches your child again he'll never live to see himself in training pants.

B. Realize that this is part of growing up and that there are children in life who might even surpass little Henry in daily activities.

C. Rush home with Henry and threaten to take away his Big Bird puppet unless he's walking by 8:00 P.M. that very evening.

D. Pull Henry out of the play group until he can sufficiently beat the pulp out of Clifford himself.

If you answered with either choice A, C or D, you have reacted appropriately for a new parent. If you selected choice B, you're either a graduate student in child psychology or have watched too many "Leave it to Beaver" reruns.

Kid Comparative Syndrome, ugly as it is, doesn't stop when precious Henry walks. Hearing your child's first intelligible words is a dramatic breakthrough for any parent whether it's their first kid or number seven. Imagine the delight, the amazement Mrs. Finegold must feel when little eighteen month old Charlie says, "Me wanna drink, Ma Ma." Mrs. Einstein couldn't have been prouder of her darling Albert when he rattled off his theory of relativity. Now just try to imagine the horror when Mrs. Finegold called her best friend Shirley to tell her the incredible news about Charlie. Shirley's sixteen month old daughter Vanessa answers the phone and articulates in flawless King's English that her mother is unavailable to talk at the moment but could she relay a message? Poor Mrs. Finegold, caught in the grip of Kid Comparative Syndrome, soon discovers she has a bit of a dark side when she silently wishes precious Vanessa a diaper rash on every square millimeter of her angelic body.

As your child grows older and he or she does indeed catch up with his peers in the walking and talking business "K C S" shows up in other ominous ways. Take the kindergarten school play for example. Your little Gloria has been singing "Somewhere Over the Rainbow" since she was three. Her two long auburn braids dance on her slender shoulders and she named her pet terrier Toto. Her favorite dress is a darling blue checked gingham jumper and she is never without her ruby red Ked sneakers. If Gloria had been around sixty years ago, Judy Garland would have been out of a job. So who does the kindergarten teacher pick to be Dorothy in the spring musical, "The Wizard of Oz?" That freckled face little snob with the punk haircut, Amanda Nelson, who wouldn't recognize the Tin Man if she ran into him in a scrap yard. Once again you have a decision to make on how to deal with this volatile situation:

A. You could cheerfully approach the music director and calmly inquire if her decision in this matter is final. If she answers yes, you smile, thank her and proceed to hire the finest criminal attorney money can buy.

B. You might mail a letter to Mr. and Mrs. Nelson informing them that if they ever want to see their daughter reach the first grade they should leave the country immediately.

C. You could gently explain to Gloria that there might be just the slightest possibility that Amanda could do a better job as Dorothy and perhaps it would be nice if she would congratulate Amanda on getting the part.

D. You could torch the school.

Obviously choice C is totally out of the question and need not be discussed further. Choice D is chancy since committing arson carries with it the penalty of incarceration, something to avoid at all costs. Choice B has strong possibilities assuming Amanda's parents are the type of folks who are receptive to a little friendly blackmail. That leaves choice A as your best shot. A requires a healthy amount of cash if a lengthy trial against the music director, school and superintendent is looming in the future. However it is imperative to look at the long range outcome of this financial expenditure. So what if you have to double mortgage the house and sell the silverware to pay for the astronomical legal fees? It will all be worth it when the school lights dim, the curtain goes up and your little princess Gloria skips along the Yellow Brick Road of the Emerald City. Kid Comparative Syndrome? It'll get you every time.

The Baby Book

Keeping accurate records of your baby's progress varies from parent to parent. Generally speaking the more organized an individual is in daily life, the more impressive baby book he or she will maintain. However regardless of one's organizational skills, one thing holds true for virtually every parent. It can all be summed up in the following rule of thumb: As each new child enters the family unit, the baby book gets progressively smaller.

Allow me to illustrate. Your basic baby book is a fifty page volume created for the sole purpose of recording important events in your new child's life. Each page has a heading such as "Homes your child has lived in." The record keeper will then use this page to list the locations and type of dwellings little Johnny has grown up in throughout his childhood. Other pages are devoted to physical development skills such as walking, talking and spitting up. There are envelopes attached to enclose clippings from Johnny's first haircut, his first lost tooth and for his college S.A.T. scores. Towards the back of the book are ten or more plastic coated pages reserved for photographs of your child taken at different stages throughout his early years.

Now that you understand the purpose of the book let me explain to you how each child's baby book will differ depending on his placement within the family. My friend Harriet displays excellent signs of what I call Baby Book Neurosis Syndrome or "BBNS." Her first child, Elliot, entered the world on March 28th, 1974 at 8:11 A.M. Eastern Standard Time. He tipped the scales at a robust eight pounds 13 ounces and was in the ninetieth percentile for height and head size. By the time Elliot was one hour old and still in the recovery room with his mom, the first two pages of his baby book had been filled in by proud dad. His vital statistics were recorded, signatures of the entire medical staff were registered, copies of his hand and foot prints were obtained and nearly two dozen Polaroid pictures of baby Elliot spanning his fascinating activities over the past fifty-eight minutes were entered in the book. Dad is positive without a doubt that his new son flashed his first smile at age sixteen minutes so he quickly filled in that historic event as well. The next day Mom carefully places Elliot's foreskin in a ziplock bag and tapes it lovingly onto the page in the baby book labeled "Traumatic Experiences for Baby." Every relative, friend, neighbor and lab technician who enters the hospital room is requested to sign the book and jot down their first impressions of baby Elliot. Each gift down to the last bonnet and bootie is recorded for future reference. By the time this kid leaves the hospital two days later, more information is available about him in this book than about the entire race of the Neanderthal man. Harriet is obsessed with the maintenance of this baby book, registering each and every burp, gurgle and drunken step of her firstborn. In fact she has so much information to provide about Elliot's activities that she must purchase additional looseleaf inserts to add to the bulging volume.

Now here's where the entire picture begins to shift. Enter child number two four years later. Sheldon is an adorable baby boy. As Harriet holds her second child in her loving arms some three weeks after his birth she says to her husband, "You know dear, maybe we should buy a baby book for Sheldon?" So a few days later the book is purchased and one afternoon when four month old Sheldon is napping Harriet opens up page one. She knows that Sheldon weighed seven pounds something but she can't quite recall the exact number of ounces. So she takes an educated guess and scribbles seven pounds, 6 ounces. Whereas in Elliot's book she wrote a four page saga on the mystery of childbirth and her maternal fortitude, in Sheldon's book she thought for a moment and wrote, "It hurt like hell." As time went on she kept up her notations on Sheldon's development but was a little vague on detail. Elliot took his first step at age eleven months, four days, six hours and forty-four minutes, his book said. Sheldon took his initial stroll somewhere between twelve to nineteen months. Pictures of Sheldon were certainly available but not at minute to minute intervals as in Elliot's book. Rather, we see a photo of newborn Sheldon on one page and on the next he's already two years old. So although there are only two children in the family, we already see a pattern developing in the area of baby book record keeping.

Now comes the drastic change. Two years after Sheldon, baby Benjamin arrives on the scene. The only reason Benjamin even has a baby book is because Aunt Martha thought to buy one. On the vital statistics page it simply says, "Big enough." To read this book thirty-five years later it would appear that little Benjamin never learned to walk, talk or ingest food. There are three documents enclosed in his book: his birth certificate, his college diploma and his divorce settlement papers. Needless to say, Harriet has become a bit lax in her child recording skills. If she had gone on to have a fourth baby, there would be absolutely no written or photographic proof of this child's existence.

Before we leave the subject of the baby book it is important to point out the fact that there is certainly no correlation in the amount of love one has for a child and the size of his baby book. Obviously Harriet loved all her sons with equal fervor. But she quickly realized that like most great novels, the first book is always the best. The sequels rarely live up to the original.

Red Alert:
Junior's Walking!

I wrote in an earlier chapter of the phenomenon called Kid Comparative Syndrome or "K C S." Nowhere can you find a better example of "K C S " than in the area of walking. Somehow accomplishing this particular activity is the granddaddy of them all when comparing your darlings to every other kid at the day care center. I can spot a first time parent one hundred crib lengths away simply by observing the reaction while they are watching their toddler's first steps. You see it's only human nature that a novice mom or dad would be ecstatic the day little Megan takes her first wobbly stab at walking. Chances are pretty good the grandparents will be summoned immediately, all out of town friends and relatives will be informed of the recent development in a family newsletter and, depending on the family's clout in the local community, an announcement will be made of Megan's feat on the 10:00 P.M. newscast.

What poor Megan's parents don't yet realize, however, is that by learning to walk, Megan's status in the family unit has been unalterably changed from innocent precious baby to toddler from hell. That sweet little bundle who was once content to lie

**When your child learns to walk, his status in the family has been
unalterably changed from innocent precious baby to toddler from hell.**

in her bassinet for one and a half hours mesmerized by her
"Sesame Street" mobile is now climbing out of that same crib
four minutes after she is put down for her afternoon nap. That
same cherubic angel who would sit contentedly for fifty-three

minutes in her playpen and gnaw on a yellow lego block is now stacking twenty-five of these babies together so she can hike herself up and swiftly scale the protective mesh webbing. Megan's mom and dad are not rocket scientists but certainly are sharp enough to realize that perhaps this walking business wasn't all it was cracked up to be. Suddenly Megan's caretakers have tripled both their work and stress levels.

Second time parents already knew what Megan's are just discovering. The later a child walks, the easier your life will be. That explains why when Megan's mom brags to her friends that her baby has begun to walk, the childless buddies Ooh and Aah while the ones who have already experienced parenthood will pat her back and offer their heartfelt sympathies. They are wise enough to know that no knick knack is safe anymore from Megan's reach. No shelf is high enough and no safety gate protective enough to keep Megan from destroying any object in her path.

To put this into perspective, if Magic Johnson can't reach it on a step ladder or Arnold Schwarzenegger can't ram his way into it, the area might be babyproof. (Always keep in mind that the key word in the previous sentence is "might.") When a toddler walks, twenty-four hour a day security is required. There can be no punching a time clock on this job, fella. It's round the clock action 365 days a year. And it's time for stair gates, closet locks, electrical outlet coverings, and hiding all breakables, or as some call it, "child proofing the house."

An amazing thing happens when little Megan's mom brings home baby brother Melvin. When he shows signs of crawling we note a slightly apprehensive look on Mom's face. When Melvin reaches up to retrieve a toy on the coffee table at nine months, Mom gently whisks him away and quickly gets her son the toy he wants. At ten months when the little angel is found standing in his crib hanging on to the side slats, Mom scoops him up and warns him if he attempts to stand up once more he'll never see Barney the Dinosaur alive again. She loses it altogether when Melvin takes his first legitimate step on his first birthday. In front of all the party guests she threatens to dip into his college fund unless he sits down and doesn't get up again for seven months. Needless to say angelic Melvin cocks his head, shrugs his little shoulders and proceeds to stroll out of the room and head directly for the glass cabinet which houses Mom's priceless crystal collection.

So to wrap up this business of walking, simply keep in mind this basic rule of thumb. Assuming your baby is in good working order, walking, like most everything else, will happen when the kid is ready for it to happen. But only a parent of one or more children truly understands why in this particular case earlier is not necessarily better.

Toilet Training: The Mega Challenge

If there ever was a true Catch 22 in child rearing, it has to be in the area of toilet training. Permit me to explain. Baby Felix is two and a half years old. For the past thirty months he has worn approximately seven thousand four hundred and fifty diapers, give or take a few hundred. If they were of the disposable variety they made a considerable dent in the city landfill as well as in the family pocketbook. If they were cloth diapers the cost and time to maintain them was pretty respectable as well. Therefore, for environmental and cost factors alone, it appears that the time has come to think about getting Felix out of diapers and into the Fruit of the Loom generation. The Catch 22 comes into play when the trainers soon realize that their own lives are affected in more ways than the actual trainees. Traveling from point A (point A being diapers) to point Z (point Z being toilet trained) is one of life's most challenging journeys seeing that 24 letters (including B.M.) lie between you and your ultimate goal. When that goal is finally reached, the trainer often finds herself asking philosophical questions such as "Was staying dry really worth all of this?"

Returning to baby Felix, Mom has decided, along with

some gentle coaxing from Grandma for the better part of ten months, to start the training process. The first thing she realizes is that she must come up with a word or phrase that Felix can understand which refers to his bodily functions. Because this is such a critical decision she wants Felix's Dad in on the naming process. After bantering back and forth for several hours it is agreed that "making puddles" will signify the wet job while the dirty work will be referred to as "mudpies." Before we continue I should note that these terms should be chosen with a great deal of thought and examination for one simple reason. These names will not end with Felix and his siblings, but will probably be passed on from generation to generation. In other words, if Felix is conditioned to produce puddles and mudpies in the toilet when he's a little kid, chances are pretty good that thirty years down the road his two children will be using the same expressions during their own training stint. So I repeat, do not make this decision in haste!

It is crucial to also remember that this is one area of child upbringing that you should not brag about to the relatives until a substantial amount of time has passed in between "accidents". Unlike other learned skills such as walking and talking, mastering toilet training is a completely different animal. For example, it's a fairly safe guess that when baby Felix learned to walk, his crawling days were pretty much a thing of the past. When he pointed to Dad and shouted, "da-da," we could assume that the vocabulary genes were finally kicking in. But when darling baby Felix wakes up from his nap one day and his diaper is dry, assuming the kid is trained is like saying Elizabeth Taylor has finally settled down in a marriage. Needless to say Felix has to prove himself over a far more respectable amount of time than one two-hour nap slot. Normally to declare the mission a success a period of at least six dry months is necessary. One note of caution, however. If you ever want a sure fire way to reverse the successful training process you and your child are in the midst of, simply pick up the phone, call someone, and tell them your kid is toilet trained. I will guarantee you without fail that within the next twelve hours your child will have an accident in his pants. It makes no difference if this kid has stayed dry for four months or four years. If you brag about it, it's all over. I am so thoroughly convinced of this phenomenon that I refuse to tell even my own mother that her youngest granddaughter is toilet trained and she's thirteen years old.

For anyone who has been a trainer, they can certainly relate to the massive amount of time and work entailed in this endeavor. These include:

- Sitting for hours on the side of the tub reading to Johnny while he wiggles on the potty.
- Bribing him with M & M's each time he clutches his groin and clapping like a wild man when he stays dry for more than fifteen minutes at a stretch.
- Demonstrating to him how you do it only to discover that after you've hiked up your own pants you head for the M & M jar yourself.

One deranged toy manufacturer even invented a "Potty Dolly" who wets when placed on its own enclosed toilet seat. Call me odd but I can only think of one thing worse than a toddler who dribbles down her leg when she walks: that is a dribbling toddler with a dribbling doll.

When you do finally hear the magic words you've been striving for, "I gotta go!" it is always in one of the three following settings:

1. After you have bundled him up in snow pants, boots, ski jacket, mittens, scarf and stocking cap

2. When you are on the busiest freeway in your city at afternoon rush hour

3. While you are at the shopping mall and the closest bathroom is eight floors down

So what can you do? Every child rearing book you ever read universally agreed that it is critical to act upon a child's request to use the bathroom. You'll defeat the very purpose of toilet training if his urgent appeal is denied. So you unbundle the kid, or exit off the frontage road, or unlawfully steer the stroller on the escalator and whisk the little tyke to the bathroom only to hear him say, "I don't hafta go anymore." One can only imagine the reaction you'll get from other people in the bathroom when they see a grown adult screaming and crying, "But you promised you'd make a mudpie!"

Recognizing Life's Key People

If one were to ask a childless person the following question, "Whom do you regard as the most important person in the world?", chances are pretty good you'll hear responses like the president of the United States, Albert Einstein, or his eminence the Pope. With sincere apologies to Mr. President, Albert, and his Holiness, when a new parent is asked this same question, if they are totally honest with themselves, they will agree it is the babysitter. The caretaker of your child might be known by various titles. The simple and most common term is babysitter. Other names include housekeeper, nanny, and au pair for those who favor a European flair. I personally prefer "Your Highness." It's a difficult concept for intelligent adults to grasp, but basically their destiny is often in the hands of an acne faced seventeen year old with a mouth full of braces and rubber bands. Whether or not you are able to attend the hospital charity ball, the movie downtown or the new Italian restaurant everyone is raving about depends solely upon the whims of this adolescent with the mousy brown hair. You still marvel at your amazing luck in finding Gertrude. She might be the kid three houses down the block, a young niece of one of your

Trust me when I warn you that the words "sharing" and "babysitter" must never be uttered in the same sentence.

business associates or the summer lifeguard at the community pool.

However you might have acquired her, there are certain

basic rules every parent needs to know regarding the babysitter business. First and undoubtedly the most essential point to remember is under no circumstances do you ever give this babysitter's name to anyone else with children living within a one hundred mile radius of your home. I don't want to appear cruel here since I know many of you were taught at an early age to participate in the act of sharing. However, trust me when I warn you that the words "sharing" and "babysitter" must never be uttered in the same sentence. I don't care if your best friend, younger sister, or Mother Teresa herself asks you for your sitter's name and number. This information must remain strictly confidential and guarded like the entrance to Buckingham Palace. Once again I don't mean to come off as sounding cynical but I can almost guarantee you that if you do break down and offer Gertrude's phone number to your closest friend on earth, this friend will do an about face and wage a salary bidding war the likes of which has never been seen before. In addition you'll find yourself calling Gertrude on a Monday for the following Saturday night only to discover that your "best friend" has already hired her for the next twelve consecutive weekends. So I repeat, sharing is for recipes and cups of sugar. Never for babysitters.

There is another critical item to keep in mind when hiring a babysitter. Never find a pretty one. Do you honestly believe that Margo, the blonde perky sophomore with the tight jeans and flawless smile, is ready to spend endless weekend evenings cleaning up after your two little precious angels? Afraid not. This kid's just biding her time until a better offer rolls around. And when I say a better offer, I am not referring to another babysitting job, but rather a hormone call from the opposite sex. I realize it can be rather touchy when advertising for a babysitter with the right qualifications.

> WANTED: A loving babysitter to watch two small children on Saturday evenings. Must have own transportation and a face that could stop a clock.

Obviously you have to be extremely cautious in making your requirements clear. The guidelines on job discrimination are mighty tough these days.

The final recommendation I would make when dealing with babysitters is to be generous with both your compliments and gift giving, and of course paying all relevant taxes in case you or your spouse plan to enter politics. Everyone in any line of work responds positively to back patting. Since your babysitter has become your most valued employee, certainly do not be stingy with your praise for her. Build up her ego. Tell her that the children include her in their bedtime prayers each night. Reassure her that no one can even come remotely close in duplicating her skill at making a frozen pizza. Warmly share with her that if she ever left you before the children could stay by themselves, the city would witness the largest breach of contract lawsuit in history. Remember, be subtle but concise. Regarding the gift giving angle, there is a simple term that can be used to describe the process perfectly: Bribery. I know you're all reading this in disgust and saying to yourself, "How low and deceitful can this woman stoop?" The answer to your question is, "As low as it will take to assure me a quality babysitter on Saturday night." Now I'm not suggesting that you go and relinquish half of your corporation's net earnings to keep your babysitter in your employment. Why should I when she would probably be content with 100,000 common shares of the company stock and a lifelong health insurance plan. If this seems a bit extravagant for you, certainly do not forget this savior on her birthday and at holiday time with some token of your appreciation. Whatever you planned on spending, spend twice as much. Be clever in your gift giving. I will always remember the ingenuity of my cousin Phyllis. Desperate to hold onto Kelly, her weekly babysitter, she bought her five pricey compact discs of her favorite recording stars. Real generous, right? The ingenious part of this plan is truly comprehended when you realize that Kelly does not own a compact disc player. Phyllis, surprise, surprise, has a disc player which is so state of the art that any music lover would be nuts not to take advantage of it. So where will Kelly be listening to her new Christmas gifts? Why at Phyllis's house, naturally!

Grandparents

I do not have a medical degree nor am I a clinical behavior psychologist. However, I am convinced that when a person becomes a grandparent there is definitely some sort of chemical chromosomal transition which occurs deep within the brain cells. I am forever amazed by the massive amounts of both time and money spent by scientific researchers examining the behavior and genetic makeup of various life forms. If they truly want to study the most unique and complex creature within the animal kingdom they simply need to collect a random sampling of your basic generic grandparent. Let's examine this specimen more closely. I challenge anyone who is a grandmother not to agree that in their "totally unbiased" opinion their grandchild is without a doubt the most beautiful child who ever lived. Certainly the most dangerous question you could ever ask a grandmother is, "Do you have a picture of little Mitchell?" Does she have a picture? Does the Pope have communion wafers? No, she doesn't have a picture, she has dozens, no hundreds of pictures, and in her purse no less. And like a hostage in enemy territory you sit as she describes in book length detail each and every photograph of precious

**The most dangerous question you can ask a grandparent is,
"Do you have a picture of your grandson?"**

Mitchell. If the grandchild is still a toddler, consider yourself fortunate. The slide presentation might be over in as little as two hours. However, if little Mitchell is in his junior year at Yale, cancel all your appointments for the next two weeks. She has a lot of ground to cover.

Not only does every grandparent in existence have the most gorgeous grandchild the world has ever seen but strangely enough this same child just happens to be the smartest one since Einstein, as well. No, I take that last part back. Their grandchild is indeed smarter that even old Albert himself. You, the father of darling four month old Veronica, call your mother and tell her that last night her precious little grand-daughter took her first wobbly attempt at crawling from one corner of the playpen to another. That same afternoon at her weekly bridge game Veronica's grandma interrupts her part-ner's bid by announcing, "I think you should all be aware that last night my new granddaughter walked unassisted from the kitchen to her bedroom." And then there's the case where four year old Marvin pointed out the word "stop" on a road sign when driving with his grandmother one afternoon. Was Grandma impressed, you ask? Just ask her canasta club. "My little Marvin knows how to read, you know. He'll be starting War and Peace next week."

You'll notice other "subtle" changes in people when they be-come grandparents. Do you remember your own dad's reac-tion when you asked him for that train set you wanted so des-perately when you were nine years old? It probably went something like this: "Are you out of your mind or something? Do you think I have a money tree growing in the back yard?" Enter the same man, now a grandfather, twenty-five years later. "Grandpa, my dad won't buy me my own Nintendo set and it only costs $159.95." Guess who suddenly found that money tree growing in his yard? Yup, good old Grandpa. The same guy who three decades ago was preaching to you about the value of a dollar was now shopping with his grandson, check-book in hand. And do you remember when you begged your mother to buy you those great duck boots that absolutely everyone but you were wearing? And she told you that the boots you had were perfectly adequate and scolded you for being such a "clothes horse." This very woman just took your eleven year old Brian to the shoe store and bought him a pair of tennis shoes with a price tag so high you contemplated listing them on your home owners insurance policy. Go figure it out. As your parents they were Mr. and Mrs. "We did it the old fashioned way. We earned it!" They become grandparents and, Abrakadabra, it's as if they all have hidden Swiss bank accounts and a forest of money trees.

There is one other fascinating observation one can make when studying the psyche of grandparents. In their eyes it is not even remotely possible that their grandchild could do anything wrong without a very logical explanation. Little Helga threw a temper tantrum in the grocery store today? "She's just a little tired," says Grandma. Dumpling-faced Donald hit Angela in the head with his Big Wheel riding car during recess? "I'm sure she hit him first, that little tramp," defends Grandpa. To a grandparent there is always a legitimate alibi. God help the person who would even dare suggest that perhaps their little grand angels would somehow be the culprits in any situation. I think my favorite story about grandparent loyalty has to be the one in which a twenty-eight year old man was at a pretrial hearing in which he was accused of robbery and attempted assault with a deadly weapon. After the judge read the long list of charges against the man, the defendant's grandmother stood up in the crowded courtroom and pleaded, "But your honor, he must have been teething at the time."

Once a Parent,
Always a Parent

ittle Sally just had her fourth birthday and baby Freddie
is now 18 months old. You are a stay-at-home mom and
except for an occasional Saturday night out and your
weekly book club meeting, your life for the past year and a half
has been basically diapers, ear infections and fantasies of making wild passionate love with Mister Rogers. You and your husband have planned a ten day Mexican holiday for the past six
months. Grandma has offered her services as a babysitter, the
boss has given his blessing and you've read every article ever
printed on how to add that renewed spark to your marriage
after the kids come.

As you await your departure you dream of lazy afternoons
on a sandy beach, romantic conversations beneath a star filled
Acapulco sky and long extended dinners where the two of you
can nourish one another's souls with words of love and desire.
You are so caught up with the rapture of the moment, you forget that anyone or anything else matters to you besides your
love. You are prepared to completely wipe from your memory
any traces of your real life and the responsibilities demanded of
you. Sounds beautiful, right? Straight out of Shakespeare.

Newsflash! I hate to interrupt you, Romeo and Juliet, but as picture perfect as this little scenario sounds, the following situation is more likely to occur. After a tearful farewell at home you head to the airport for your dream vacation. You settle yourself in your airplane seat, order a cocktail, look into your beloved's eyes and softly murmur, "Did you remember to empty the diaper pail before we left?" Your loved one strokes your arm, undresses you with his eyes and responds, "Yes, darling, but I think I left a particularly messy one soaking in the downstairs toilet." And so begins your ten day adventure into Paradise. Do you know what the nine most often spoken words are on a parent's vacation? "What do you think the kids are doing now?" Yes, the very same people who fantasized about ten days away from the kids spend every waking moment talking, worrying and wondering about them. Remember those romantic dinners you dreamt about? You know, the ones where you were the only two people on earth? Surprise, surprise! Guess who quietly crept into 99% of the conversation? You got it! Good old Sally and Freddie. And remember those dreamy afternoons you were going to spend on those warm Mexican beaches? Forget it. After thirty minutes, one of you will break down and suggest a shopping trip into the city to buy Sally a pinata or Freddie some bongo drums. You sip Margaritas and discuss teething in hushed tones. Dancing beneath the moonlight you gaze at one another and lovingly discuss what could possibly be the cause for Freddie's little rash behind his left testicle. Without realizing it you have unfolded the dinner napkin, unwrapped the straw and cut up the meat of the stranger sitting at the table next to you.

So what's the moral of this little tale, you ask? Simply, if you thought you could stop thinking and acting as a parent just because you were thousands of miles away from the kids, forget it. Regardless of the child's sex, age and maturity level, a kid will always be a kid in your eyes. For parents there is no such thing as a kid too old to protect and nurture.

Some mothers can overdo it, however. Take the case of Harold, who had an extremely over protective mother. He became an astronaut who eventually participated in the United States space shuttle program. Harold and six other astronauts were selected to fly on a scientific space mission recently. When pictures from space were radioed back to the Kennedy Space Center it was very obvious which one of the floating astronauts was Harold. He was the one carrying the sweater.

Straight Talk About Feeding The Kids

D o you recall my earlier comments on the upkeep of your child's baby book? The one that shows a definite correlation between a child's placement in the family unit and the amount of historical information collected on him or her? To refresh your memory: the first and therefore oldest offspring has enough photos and data collected to fill a room at the Smithsonian Institution in Washington. When these same parents are asked for a recent photo of their fourth child, who is now in junior high school, they still pull out the hospital mug shot taken three hours after the kid's birth. Always keep in mind it's not that they loved number four child any less than number one. It's just that somewhere along the way they got a bit lazy and less compulsive about the whole process. Well, this phenomenon doesn't just occur in this particular area of child rearing. One can also witness this trend in the nutritional upbringing of your children, as well. Ok. I hear gasps of skepticism all over the place with this remark. Don't think I don't know what you're saying to yourself. "Is this woman actually suggesting that a child is fed differently depending on their numerical placement in the family?" My answer to you is an emphatic, "You bet your organically-grown green beans on it. Or, if in the case of the third or fourth child, you can bet your Hostess Ding Dongs on it."

Situation in point: Virginia and Howard are a lovely couple who met in a most interesting way. After a strenuous three hour workout with individual trainers, they both enjoyed a vegetable packed muscle building drink at the health club's fitness bar. Over the crowd in a sweat filled room Howard spotted beautiful Virginia. He was enticed by the sensual manner in which her carrot juice dribbled seductively down her dimpled chin. Making his way over to her table, he struck up a conversation about the perils of preservatives in foods, and the rest was history. Their romance flourished as they shared their life's interest with one another. They explored the mysteries of grains and legumes together. They unabashedly spoke of oat bran and carotene replacement therapy. While in the throes of passion Howard would softly whisper sweet endearments like low density Lipoprotein Lipasc in Virginia's ear. They knew they were the closest two people could ever become when they shared their most passionate of all secrets; their cholesterol levels. And so Howard and Virginia married and vowed to love each other through health and more health as long as they both shall live. They chose to drop the "through sickness" part since they knew it would never apply to them as long as they maintained their current eating standards.

Two years later Virginia became pregnant with their first child. When baby Derrick arrived, you can just about imagine the nutritional life of this child. While other babies were sipping canned apple juice from their bottles, Derrick was chugging a mixture of natural zucchini and squash extract. When other toddlers were lapping down jars of Gerber's strained peaches, Virginia was at the health food co-op buying pesticide free Chilean grapes to throw in her food processor for her chemically free son. And when Virginia was out and saw other

**Baby number one: "Preservatives shall never pass
my darling baby's lips."**

mothers give their two year olds a cookie or a doughnut, it was all she could do to keep from calling the child protection agency to report these negligent parents.

Three years later, little Derrick became a big brother to baby Dougie. Life became a little more complicated for Virginia and

Baby number three: "I don't care what the fat content of a pepperoni pizza is. Just buy it and get it here quick!"

Howard. They're both working full time and their parenting chores have suddenly doubled. Virginia doesn't quite have the time anymore to shop for the essence of squash vitamin that she religiously administered to Derrick on a daily basis, so she settles for artifically colored cherry vitamins instead, even though they might have just the slightest trace of carcinogenic red food coloring. The puree cycle on her food processor is not working just right so she breaks down and gives Dougie what the other 98% of the nation's babies are thriving on: Gerber's strained meats and vegetables. Dougie threw a bit of a temper tantrum in the market last week. Glancing about for fear of being discovered, Howard buys him a sugar cookie at the bakery counter to keep him quiet. These are all subtle changes, mind you, but could the guru couple of health be letting down their guard, perhaps?

Another member, Joey, joins the family two years later. Virginia is now vice president of marketing and Howard seems to be traveling a bit more in his job. As they madly dash about the kitchen getting ready for work, Virginia hastily makes breakfast for the two older boys. Sugar Coated Fruity Pebbles and sweet rolls. They run out of milk for their cereal so Virginia substitutes Mountain Dew. As she flies out the door she tells the babysitter to take Joey to McDonalds' for lunch and to pick up pepperoni pizza for their dinner later that evening. So you see, Virginia and Howard tried their best. They didn't love Joey any less than their other two boys. Life just got a bit more complicated, that's all. And they finally came to grips with the fact that preservatives can not only lengthen the shelf life of food, but perhaps your sanity as well. Remember Chilean grape eating little Derrick? Well, he's a great kid and has a slew of close friends. They particularly enjoy coming over to his house after school. The chocolate milk and Little Debbie cakes always hit the spot.

Helping With Homework

Helping your children with their homework, regardless of their age is perhaps one of the most dangerous of all parental tasks. For you see up until the homework stage of life, parents can just about successfully bluff their way through any situation and there's a pretty reasonable chance that their kid will believe them. But when you know that the geography or math teacher is ultimately going to be critiquing the answers you help your child with, your credibility is suddenly up for grabs.

Obviously it stands to reason that the younger your child is the easier your job will be to assist him with his schoolwork. Although it's rather rare to see a nursery school or kindergarten teacher assign homework, occasionally you will come across a situation where a preschool teacher is really a frustrated college professor in disguise and insists on after hour assignments from tykes who can barely manage to tie their own shoe laces. Their "homework" is really just fun little art projects where they have to paste roofs onto houses and color flower petals with magic marking pens. If the teacher is more academically inclined she'll ask her students to match up color names with the appropriate hue from their eight count box of crayons. Take advantage of these years, parents. When your kids are in these very early formative stages they look upon you as brain surgeons. Now is the time to really impress these little people because you may never intellectually look this good again. Dazzle them with your ability to count to thirty. Hypnotize them with your amazing skill of reciting the alphabet while hopping on one foot. When Erma is six years old she'll never be able to detect whether you received advanced degrees in political science or if you were a fifth grade drop out. At this age the most appropriate adjective to describe you is simply brilliant.

When your child is in first and second grade the real "meat" of her education has begun. Now you could assume that since you are actually reading this book, you are capable of helping your child with any reading homework he might have. This is probably a safe bet if all you need to do is actually look at the words in your child's book and help him sound them out when he gets stumped. However, things could start to get a little bit sticky if there are also spelling words included in the reading workbook. Although at this age you should be able to handle yourself quite efficiently, there will be one or two occasions where you might slip up with a trick question of when to use the words to, too and two. It's an honest mistake and the kid is still young enough to believe you when you tell him he heard you wrong and put down an incorrect answer. At this age math should still be within your comprehension although inwardly you might feel a bit uneasy over the fact that two of the simple addition problems you helped your child with came back marked wrong. Again, at this tender age of life you will still have enough clout with your child to convince him that he simply misunderstood you and that is why one or two answers might be in error.

All parents are faced with the situation they dread but know they must confront eventually; the day their child comes home with schoolwork that they cannot help them with. Obviously this situation will differ from parent to parent depending on their own level of intellect. For some the dark day of infamy will come over a spelling lesson. For others the ceiling will cave in when their kid starts to learn fractions and decimal points.

For me, my Achilles heel was geography. Up until my daughter was in fourth grade I had sailed through her homework sessions. I was a regular Eleanor Roosevelt breezing through reading, spelling, and long division. Granted I did come across a minor roadblock with fractions but I cleverly concealed my ignorance and simply shifted this duty to her mathematically-inclined father without raising any suspicions on her part. And then it happened. The geography lesson that blew my cover and my credibility. Each child was given a map of the United States and asked to fill in the names of the fifty states in the appropriate places. The exercise was to be done on the honor system meaning that each child had promised to do the work without the aid of a textbook or globe. My daughter asked me for help. I looked at the map and quickly detected a noticeable increase in my heart rate. A slight film of perspiration covered 80% of my body and my hand holding the map quivered with a personality of its own. She finally had me. I suppose I could take comfort in the fact that I lasted longer than some of the other parents. My friend Faye only made it to the third grade before her son Lucas discovered his mom didn't know the difference between a dividend and a divisor. And then there was poor Lucile. Distinguishing a noun from a verb cut her down in the prime of life when her little Martin was only in second grade. So there I was clutching the map of the United States, looking into the eyes of my daughter who up until then had no reason to doubt my scholastic ability and proceeded to completely destroy the upstanding academic reputation I had successfully built up over the past four years.

**Take advantage of your kid's early school years.
You may never look this brilliant again.**

Under my guidance Seattle, Washington, was now perched next to Florida, Rhode Island neighbored California and the Lone Star state of Texas hovered somewhere between Minnesota and Iowa. Not since the Civil War had the map of the U.S. been destroyed so violently. There was absolutely nothing I could say to my daughter to clear my name. In one brief moment it was apparent to her that maybe mom wasn't quite as brilliant as she once appeared to be.

I know I have no one to blame but myself. I simply chose the wrong "homework path." You see, there are three paths a parent can choose when handling a homework assignment they know is above their heads. Path A, the road I regrettably chose, is when a parent decides that regardless of their own skill level they are determined to help their child with their homework even at the cost of permanent damage to their reputation. I like to think of it as betting all of your money on the final "Jeopardy" question when the topic is Ancient Lithuanian Artifacts. Path B is when the parent knows he doesn't have a clue to what a particular homework assignment is but is clever enough to cover his stupidity with psychological mind games. For example, if a parent is completely at a loss over a math assignment a Path B response would be, "Arthur, I could easily show you how to find the common denominator of this fifteen digit number to the eighth power and multiply it by itself times four squared, but if I did, you would never learn how to do it yourself and I would have miserably failed you as a parent." Arthur might be upset that he has to figure this out by himself, but your credibility is still safely intact. Path C is the option least taken by parents due to the destructive nature on one's ego. This is when a parent will study a sheet of homework, look the child squarely in the eyes, and say, "I don't know how to do this." The silence is deafening. You can't believe you said it. Your kid can't believe you said it. You may never be quite this vulnerable again. Could it be possible? The same man who runs a company of three hundred employees in two different states actually is stumped by a sixth grade spelling word? The woman they call mom who has aspirations to be mayor can't name the world's continents? Path C is a tough path to choose but in the end will save much of the needless embarrassment encountered on Path A, the one most traveled by parents who are unwilling to risk their credibility.

If you are still choosing Path A by the time your child enters high school it is crucial to remember this one thing. It is imperative that you keep up with your child's homework from the very first day of school. Unless you have personally received the Nobel prize for scientific research it will literally be an impossibility to pick up your son's chemistry textbook in the middle of December and understand what is going on in class. Even if the kid never asks for your help until the last week in February, if you haven't read along since Day one, you can forget about ever solving a problem by Day three or four. High school students are mighty perceptive and will probably not buy the Path B technique at this age. So if you want to make life a whole lot easier for yourself you can do one of two things at this point in your child's education. You can choose ego busting Path C or you can take the super chicken way out. You can enroll your child in the school's foreign exchange program. That way some unfortunate set of parents in Denmark or Uruguay can deal with your kid's homework and you come out smelling like a rose.

Crime and Punishment: Junior the Hard Core Felon

To scold or not to scold. To spank or not to spank. Parents have been stumped by these questions and others like them ever since the Neanderthal man caught his tykes playing with fire in the back of the family cave. As in just about every other area of child rearing, parents tackle the discipline dilemma in the manner they feel is best for their own individual child. However different one parent's method of discipline is compared to another, there is one universal feature that every parent on the face of this earth practices at one time or another: the use of ridiculous and totally absurd threats to a disobedient child.

Let's take a look at one of the most commonly used but worthless threats administered to a kid. Thirteen year old Christopher has tried his mother's patience all day. He left his dirty dishes on the breakfast room table, spilled root beer on the silk oriental throw rug, didn't bother to call home when he went to Howard's house after school, and for the third time in a week forgot to bring his math homework home. Christopher's mom graduated magna cum laude from Brown University, majoring in child psychology. She carefully evaluates the situation and in her educated manner determines that the proper punishment for her son's delinquent behavior is a four hour stretch in his room alone to ponder his evil ways. Sounds pretty cruel, right? A scenario right out of Attica prison. Poor, poor Christopher. A hostage in his own house. If his incarceration were any longer his story of abuse and imprisonment might be the opening segment on "Nightline." There's just one minor flaw with this discipline approach, however. It seems as if good old Christopher has a few little comforts in this prison cell known as his bedroom. An IBM top of the line computer system complete with color printer rests on top of his mahogany desk. Nestled over in one corner of the cell is a 30 inch color television with remote control. Heaven forbid the prisoner should have to strain himself by getting out of his heated waterbed to change the channel. Connected to the T.V. is a complicated array of electrical wires and cords. One belongs to the V.C.R. and the other cord snakes up to the Nintendo electronic game unit. On the opposite wall of the penitentiary is a state of the art four head C.D. player. Resting against the high intensity speakers is a metal cabinet housing well over 100 compact discs. The music is blaring so loudly that poor desolate Christopher can just barely hear his three line portable phone when it rings. To protect himself against the ravages of dehydration and starvation sometimes encountered during a prison term, there is a small seven tier shelf of Coke, Cheetos, M & M's, Twinkies, Whoppers and other provisions to see him through the long terror filled ordeal. And so this is the pathetic gut wrenching punishment dealt by mom, the warden of the big house. There's only one thing wrong with this discipline of choice. When the governor pardons Christopher after his four hour stretch in the bowels of hell the inmate is in no real hurry to leave. So obviously if you're going to use incarceration in one's room as a discipline technique, it's not going to be very effective if the little cell bears a remarkable resemblance

This is the pathetic gut wrenching punishment dealt by Mom, the warden of the Big House.

to Disneyland or Epcot. In Christopher's case, his mother would have made a significantly bigger impact if she firmly informed Christopher that because of his behavior he would not be allowed to enter his room for the afternoon. I can almost guarantee you that if Mom takes this action instead, Christopher will never be a repeat offender.

Unlike Christopher whose mom, despite the mockery of it all, carried out her threat, there are other threats made in the heat of the moment that are clearly irrational and of a completely bizarre nature. How many times have you been in a supermarket and witnessed this scene? Three year old Debbie is running in and out of the grocery aisles. Pulling canned goods off the shelves and squeezing every nectarine in the produce bin, she has quickly drawn the attention of every other shopper in the general vicinity. Frustrated to her wit's end, Mother grabs darling Debbie and screams over the noise of the store's intercom, "This is the last time I'll ever take you shopping again!" Come on now, Mother. Is this a threat you can honestly carry out? You know you're not about to leave a three year old alone in the house when you go to the market again next week. Debbie knows you're not going to leave her alone, so what good is a threat you can't possibly carry out?

While I'm on the subject of making threats you can't see through I feel I must warn you of the worst, most dangerous kind of threat of all. This is the threat you make which has the most risky repercussions to the parents themselves. An example: Your seven year old twins have been invited to a neighborhood birthday party. The parents of the birthday boy are classic masochists in that they have planned a five hour birthday extravaganza for their only child. You have been fantasizing about these five hours of freedom since the day the invitation came in the mail. The possibilities seem endless.

- Going to lunch with an old friend and not having to play tic tac toe or hangman while waiting for your meal to arrive.
- Taking in an "R" rated matinee.
- Languishing over a steamy novel that doesn't say "Golden Book" on the outside cover.

The world was for you to grasp. At least those five hours were. And then the unspeakable happens. In one brief horrific moment, you do something so incredibly stupid that it's completely off the charts on measuring one's insanity. The twins are fighting non-stop all morning. Toys are thrown, there is endless crying, and finally blood is drawn as one twin punches the other in the nose with the caboose from the electric train set. In a raging torrent of anger you scream at the top of your lungs, "That does it! You two are so terrible that you're not going to the birthday party today!"

Your words are like a hard punch in the stomach. And I don't mean the kid's stomach. You didn't really say that, did you? Please tell me you didn't just give up 300 precious minutes of parole time by that foolish threat. What do you do now? You have two clear choices to contemplate. You can show your children who the boss is in this family unit. You can prove that you are indeed a woman of your word and when you say they cannot go to the party, under no circumstances will they go to the party. Or you can completely dodge your parental responsibily as family disciplinarian, meekly murmur, "Just kidding," and send the kids to the party knowing that their mother is a spineless jellyfish of a parent. Of course it's your decision, but if they were my kids there would be no decision. As far as I'm concerned you can't put a price on freedom. Birthday party, here they come!

The oddest threat I have heard, however, is the one where the parent in complete exasperation says to his child, "If you do this your name will be mud." I never really believed that any parent would actually carry out this one until I was watching the 6:00 P.M. national news one night on television. The anchorman's name was Roger Mudd. It suddenly occurred to me that this man actually had parents who carried out the threat. To this day I often wonder what good old Roger did to deserve his name. It must have been a real humdinger.

The "Non-working Mother"

Discussing a non-working mother is like talking about non-wet water or non-fattening hot fudge sundaes. They simply do not exist. Women who choose to stay home to raise their kids need to realize two things about the society in which we live. First, despite the fact that you have elected to become a twenty-four hour nurse, educator, laundress, cook, psychologist, peace negotiator, warden, cop, seamstress, chauffeur, coach, and home maintenance engineer, when your child is asked if their mother works, the answer will invariably be "No." Secondly, once the word has gotten out that you indeed have chosen this honorable profession, you become the target for every volunteer job and committee chairmanship in your community.

Stay at home moms have children who have this annoying little habit of raising their hands in school and announcing on a regular basis, "My mom will do it!" It makes no difference that Junior offered your assistance on the horseback riding field trip and you just happen to have this little medical problem of slipping into an allergic coma when you come into direct contact with horse hair. Once he's offered your services, you're elected. No primary, no general election, you're it. After all, as long as you "don't work," why shouldn't you do it? All you need to do is hire a sitter at $4.50 an hour for the baby, cancel the appointment with the vet, reschedule the carpet cleaning service, find someone else to pick up the laundry and go grocery shopping, take Bradley to the orthodontist, organize Sandra's dancing carpool, and serve dinner to the family before you coach the girls' church softball team. What's the problem?

I hate to brag about my accomplishments in life, but I feel I must tell you about a record I have set over my twenty-two years of being a stay at home "non-working" mom. I have been a class room mother for seventeen consecutive years. Seventeen years! During this time five different presidents have lived in the White House, the Berlin Wall came down, and Michael Jackson underwent thirteen plastic surgeries. Do you have any idea of how many pitchers of Kool Aid I have seen tipped during this span of time? Do you even have the tiniest inkling of how many Rice Krispie bars I've made and Cheerio necklaces I have strung over the past seventeen years? Our Congress has been busily debating the question of whether or not we should have term limitations for certain members of our government. Trust me when I tell you that while they're at it they should limit the number of years a woman should be a room mother. It would be in the children's best interest. You see, when I was a room parent for my son in the mid 1970's I came into the classroom as a young spirited mother filled with fresh new ideas on how to bring joy, laughter and mirth into those uninhibited clear thinking first grade minds. The class parties were innovative, carefully planned to the last detail and smacked of originality and creativity. I dressed up at Halloween as Raggedy Ann, spent hours baking heart shaped sugar cookies for Valentine's Day and took the little darlings cherry picking to celebrate George Washington's birthday. When my daughter started school I attempted to be the room mother for both of my children's classes. I would get the party games in motion for my son's fourth grade class and then dash fifty yards down the hall to serve lemonade and cupcakes to the second grade. By the sixth consecutive year I began to notice a subtle change in my behavior. The class parties had gone from Hollywood extravaganzas to mildly entertaining festivals. My Halloween costume had toned down a bit, forgoing the Raggedy Ann duds for a simple witch hat and black cape. The elaborate baked goods were now store bought doughnuts and party games were kept to two or three at best. As each year rolled by, things began to decline fast. My third and youngest child is now in sixth grade. Unless mother nature pulls a fast one, this should be my swan song year as room mother. It's not a minute too soon. This year on Halloween I wore a "Jason" Friday the 13th hockey mask, threw stale Twinkies and water at the kids and warned them that if anyone smarted off I'd see to it that they were transferred to a third world country for seventh grade. Quite a change from the days when Gerald Ford was president.

As a "non-working" mother you are also open season for the jobs of den mother, Girl Scout leader, spring carnival chairman, fall talent show coordinator, vision and hearing screener, volunteer drama advisor, youth choir director, and cross country track meet timer. Your home is headquarters for the annual girl scout cookie drive, greeting card holiday fund raiser and pee wee basketball pizza banquet. Because you are home eating bon-bons and languishing in steamy bubble baths all day your friends who have a "real job" leave your number in the case of any emergency. So not only are you now on call for your own children, but for half of the neighborhood's kids as well.

My oldest childhood friend and I still keep in regular contact. Choosing to develop her professional career before tackling parenthood, she had her first child at age 39 after eighteen years of marriage. She took a three month maternity leave after her son was born. Now this is a woman who left a high powered six figure job in a huge corporation. She advised countless people each day, was chief decision maker in a large department and was a pioneer of sorts in a very specialized field of computer technology. She gave all of this up for ninety days of Pampers and Simulac. I called her dozens of times during the first month to get a status report but she could never talk more than 45 seconds. She was either feeding, changing, bathing or burping the kid. When she wasn't busy with him she was doing laundry or recording in his baby book. When I went to visit she looked like a prisoner of war who had undergone months of sleep deprivation. She threw in the towel shortly after that and returned to work two weeks early before her new job of "non-working" mom killed her. Never again did this woman ever ask another mother if she "worked."

Birthday Parties, or Scenes From Hell

Birthday parties bear a remarkable similarity to pregnancy and birth in that immediately after both events you make a solemn vow never to have another one. Fortunately, to preserve both the planet and the human species, mother nature comes to the rescue and miraculously wipes away just enough of the gory details from our memories. Regarding birthday parties, however, parents usually do remember the events from year to year but two little things called guilt and competition kick in to preserve the tradition each year.

Throwing a birthday party for your one year old is a piece of cake, no pun intended. Never again will the celebration be this easy so take advantage of it. The usual first year gala is a cozy get-together with Grandma, Grandpa, an aunt, uncle and maybe a cousin or two. Because junior still takes two naps, the party is held normally in the late afternoon or after dinner for cake and ice cream. All of the attention is focused on the birthday child and there are more video cameras going than on the night of the Grammy awards. The ratio of adults to children is about 15 to 1 if you planned it right. Before I go any further I feel that I must warn you about something that only seasoned birthday party throwers like myself would know. If you remember only one thing I am telling you about birthday parties, let it be this: once you invite a kid to a birthday party simply because he or she is the child of a good friend of yours, you can consider this a lifetime invitation. As long as this person remains your friend she will expect her kid to be a party guest forever. Whether or not your child is even remotely fond of her child is not an issue. In fact, in situations such as these your kid most likely will detest this child with a vengeance and rant and rave each year when you tell him he has to invite her. So I repeat, if your best friend Gladys has a dimple faced daughter (Lulu) who is only two months younger than your son (Irving) make darn sure you fully understand the consequences of inviting Lulu to that first birthday party. Believe me when I tell you that one day when Irving is twelve years old and wants to go to the Yankees game with ten of his boyfriends, you're going to have one heck of a time explaining the situation to Gladys.

A child's second birthday is almost as easy as the first with the exception that the kid is now walking and opening his own gifts which might make for a messier but still relatively stress-free affair. The birthday guest list, except for a babysitter or two, hasn't changed much from the year before. You may have progressed to finger sandwiches and animal shaped jello but it is perfectly acceptable to stick with the cake and ice cream cuisine if simple entertaining is your style.

Age three is when you decide to complicate matters. Chances are pretty good that by now little Irving has met a few pals at daycare or at his play group. You decide it's time to expand the birthday guest list a bit and invite five friends and, of course, Lulu, your friend Gladys' kid. At age three the parents come with their child, praise the Lord. You serve hot dogs, potato chips and red Hawaiian punch. I'd like to stop here for a moment to evaluate this move. You are a bright woman. You

**By age four you do the most dangerous thing a parent can do.
You invite the kids without their parents.**

probably graduated from high school. Some of you might even have gone on to college. Then, why, pray tell, would you serve three year old babies red Hawaiian punch? It remains as one of life's unsolved mysteries. Anyway, you made it through the party. Irving made four of the children cry, two kids threw up, one choked on a chip, and by now you'll realize you should have spent the extra $29.95 to have the family room carpet Scotch Guarded.

By age four you do the most dangerous thing a parent can do. You invite the kids without their parents. This is also the year you will witness a very interesting phenomenon. You know your friends who can never be on time to anything? They come late for lunch, they have never heard the national anthem sung at a football game, they are always the last ones through the gate when the airplane doors are closing. These very same people are the ones who drop their kids off first to a birthday party. If the invitation says 12:00, they're at the door by 11:30. However, interestingly enough, their "late genes" somehow kick back in at pick up time, as they saunter in to gather up the little darlings 45 minutes after the party's over. These children are also, oddly enough, the ones who spill everything, run 90 miles per hour through the living room, and find that little hidden video that you and your husband wickedly watch alone when the children are in bed for the night. You plan the party to last for two hours. Fifteen minutes into the ordeal you assume your watch isn't running because time can't possibly be moving this slow. You only invited ten kids but it seems as if they're multiplying before your eyes. Balloons are popping, toys are flying, and you slowly detect a rather odd aroma coming from Jimmy, the kid who lives down the street. Was he the one who gets the runs when he eats chocolate frosting? It is at this point that you make a decision. Next year's party will be out of the house.

As soon as you've decided to bring the party into outside territory you've opened yourself up to two new possible dilemmas. For one, if the little angels destroy a restaurant or video arcade you could be slapped with a pricey lawsuit. Secondly, the odds are pretty strong that if you take twelve kids to a public place, only eleven will be accounted for at the end of the party. Then you have to go through the trauma of searching for that one kid without losing the rest of the group in the process. When you finally find him he turns out to be the biggest trouble maker at the party and you secretly wish you hadn't looked so hard after all.

The older a child gets the more complicated the birthday party becomes. The competition factor kicks in big time when parents try to outdo one another's galas. The guest lists grow as your child is invited to his friends' parties. You find you can't invite only half of the third grade because you don't want any hurt feelings. Before you know it you have twenty-eight kids from school, thirteen from church, four first cousins and, of course, Lulu, the lifetime invitee. Every year you make the same speech to your child. "This is positively the last time you're having such a big party. Next year you can invite only two or three friends." I've been there many times. And do you know what you'll be doing next year at this time? Probably sitting with thirty-five fourth graders in the bleacher section at the Shrine Circus.

Parents Make the Best Actors

Being a good parent is certainly not a simple thing to master. Parenting classes offer ways to learn skills such as toilet training, health needs and effective discipline techniques. However, there is something that virtually every parent will need to know that no parenting class can teach: how to be a good actor.

Everyone has either heard or used the expression, "it's a nice baby." When you hear the word "nice" you know immediately that there is something about this kid that doesn't quite measure up. Either his ears are too big for his head, his nose resembles two garage doors in the middle of his face, or one eye is looking east while the other's glancing west. You stare at this specimen through the hospital viewing glass and know immediately that this child will have to make his livelihood in ways other than being a Gerber baby. Of course you wouldn't dare mention to anyone, least of all his parents, that this kid bears a remarkable resemblance to W. C. Fields, so you come up with "nice," the only adjective you can think of at the time. Another method people sometimes turn to in this situation is complimenting a new parent on their baby's beautiful hands. "She has the fingers of a concert pianist," is an old standby. What you are really saying is "I've seen better looking monkeys at the San Diego Zoo." This is your first stab at acting and it's not bad for your virgin try.

The true test in measuring a parent's acting ability comes when their child is about three years old. Usually the scene goes something like this. Wilbur races to meet you at the door when you come to pick him up from pre-school. He excitedly clutches a piece of paper bearing a still wet circle-shaped orange blob. With much formality he proudly thrusts the picture into your hands and awaits your reaction. You examine it, turn it 360 degrees and finally ask, "What is it?" Wilbur is aghast at your apparent ignorance. He informs you that this is a picture of Fred the family dog, sitting under the apple tree in front of his house watching a fire engine drive down the block. Acting Alert! "Why, of course, darling. I see it all now. Such detail, such action, such imagination." Such acting! You bring the picture home, ceremoniously hang it on the refrigerator and treat the kid like Leonardo da Vinci himself. The same acting artistry is required in countless areas of child rearing. When your daughter makes her first batch of chocolate chip cookies by herself, in between choking spells you tell her she bakes like Julia Child. When she dances in her annual recital, you will convince her she moves like Baryshnikov as you tape bandaids on her bloody knees. When Stewart walks after his fifth time at bat during his Little League game you hoot and holler, "Good eye, buddy. Good eye!"

My father was one of the all time greatest actors as parents go. Two memories of my childhood still stick vividly in my mind. I was in a cooking class while in junior high school back in the early 60's. Our first "project" was making baking powder biscuits. I was so proud of my first cooking endeavor that I brought home two of the biscuits for my family to sample. My dad took a bite, raved about the texture and flavor and quietly slipped out of the room. It was only later that evening when I took the kitchen trash out to the garage did I see the half eaten white hockey puck lying in the bottom of the garbage can. I also suspect that my dad might have chipped a tooth as well because I clearly remember him calling his dentist the next morning.

My Dad's acting career flourished when I was in a high school sewing class. I have always hated sewing. I have never been able to tell a dart from an inseam. During this year-long class each student was expected to sew a blouse, skirt, and jacket, in that order. By December everyone in the class had progressed to the skirt. Everyone but me, that is. I struggled along with my yellow and white gingham blouse, redoing each sleeve, stitch, and buttonhole dozens of times. By March the rest of the group had moved on to the jacket and there I was, still two garments behind everyone else. On the last day of school in June all the girls modeled their three piece ensembles while I meekly held up my still basted pitiful blouse. I didn't dare try it on for fear of sneezing and splitting the whole damn thing. The teacher took pity on me, gave me a "D" as a gift, and sent me home with the most pathetic excuse for a blouse you can imagine. I showed the final product to my dad. He took a look at it, told me it looked just like a Paris copy and went outside to wash his car. I was feeling pretty pleased about the blouse after dad's remark and I carefully laid it on the kitchen counter to show my mother when she came home. Enter dad, fifteen minutes later. He had forgotten to bring out a dry cloth to wipe off the car when he was done washing it. So he ran into the kitchen, grabbed the first rag he could find, ripped it up and went back outside. I don't need to tell you what he ripped up, do I? I knew you'd guess.

Parents are constantly being judged in their acting careers but there is one area of life that is so challenging that even Charlton Heston could have a tough time. School band concerts. Sitting through a fourth grade band concert is like no other activity in life. I've tried to think of something to compare this to such as scraping fingernails on a blackboard but even that isn't a fair comparison. You can scream and clench your ears during the blackboard incident. You can't do that during a band concert, as much as you would like to. Not only can't you scream and clench but you have to smile, nod, and applaud. Do you have any idea of the self control it takes to do this? You force yourself to think of melancholy or morbid situations to keep yourself from breaking up. Twice you've started to leave the building when you thought the fire alarm went off, only to discover it was the alto saxophone player warming up. Once the "concert" is over you rush up to your child, gather him in your arms and give the performance of the year by an actress in a leading role. "I have never heard anything so beautiful in my life! I can't believe you've only been taking lessons for two and a half months." Similar conversations are taking place throughout the gym. One parent over does it a bit and actually approaches the saxophone player for his autograph. Some people will do anything to win an Oscar.

Carpools

Parents will quickly discover that there is a direct correlation between a child's age and the amount of time which you as parent spend in your car. When your child is still an infant, her social calendar isn't exactly booked up each day. Other than trips to the daycare facility, pediatric appointments or grandma's house, your weekly time in the car is approximately two hours. Once your baby reaches toddler status you feel the time has come for some cultural enlightenment (as if she'd know the difference) so you enroll her in "Musical Trolley," a weekly 45 minute music appreciation class where fifteen two year olds scream to the beat of an instructor's bongo drums. Weekly car time is now increased to three hours. At age three your daughter begins pursuing her education in a three mornings per week nursery school half way across town. Weekly car time: Five and a half hours. By next year she is a five day a week student, has been invited to the birthday party of every kid in her class, and is now enrolled in beginning ballet, gymnastics and piano lessons. Total weekly car time is creeping towards twelve hours. If your child is involved in a sports activity you can add the following hours to your weekly time behind the steering wheel:

Baseball:	10 hours
Softball:	8 hours
Basketball:	12 hours
Football:	11 hours

Some of you might have noticed that I did not include the sport of hockey on this list. This was an intentional omission because of a very simple fact of life. Children who play hockey and parents of children who play hockey do not view this activity as simply a sport. To them hockey is a way of life, a religious cult, a total reason for being. These people eat, sleep, and breathe hockey. They are slaves to their team's "ice time" and there is virtually nothing that will come between them and the game. If hockey parents are even thinking about adding a new baby to their family, the hockey season is the perfect time to do it. Since they might have to drive their kid to practice at 2:00 A.M. (yes, A.M.) they'll be up anyway so they might as well have a newborn to feed while they're at it. (When these parents have time to conceive the kid, I don't have a clue. Perhaps between periods. Hockey periods, that is.) If an adult is a true "hockey parent" in every sense of the word then he can literally rent out his house for the duration of hockey season because if he isn't at the rink watching his kid, he will be either driving this child to or from it. To try and estimate the amount of time a hockey parent spends in his car is like trying to guess how many broken promises are made by a political candidate. It's simply an unmeasurable statistic.

There are some subtle signs you as a parent should watch for which might suggest you are spending an excessive amount of time on four wheels. First, if your weekly gasoline bill exceeds your monthly mortgage payment, you might want to reassess the situation. Another giveaway hint is when the order takers at the fast food drive through windows recognize you by voice alone. Finally, you know you've overdone the driving bit when your husband asks you to redecorate the house and you order new bucket seat covers and rear windshield wipers. You evaluate the situation and realize there are two options for you to consider. One, you can continue at this pace knowing that things will get even more frenzied once child number two and three begin their extra-curricular activities. Two, you can bite the bullet and carpool with other parents.

Now for those of you who have not had the opportunity to carpool, you're probably wondering why I seem so skeptical about the whole business. You're probably saying it seems like a logical solution to an increasing problem, right? Well, let me tell you something about carpooling. It's one of those things that looks great on paper but in reality can put you in therapy faster than you can say "strait jacket." I don't care what part of the country you are from, what nationality you claim to be, what your age is, or your financial bracket. There are certain universal problems every parent should be aware of before committing themselves to a carpool. First, every carpool ever assembled worldwide is made up of the following children:

- One who never opens his mouth
- One who never closes his mouth
- One who gets carsick on a regular basis
- One who is chronically coughing and sneezing
- Your own child

Secondly, be aware of the fact that there will always be one parent in the carpool who, without exception, will never be on time. Accept the fact that on her day to drive, your child will

**Organizing a carpool can put you in therapy faster
than you can say "strait jacket."**

be late to wherever he's going. Third, in order to qualify as a
driver in a carpool you must be virtually "shockproof" for not
only will you hear stories such as, "My mom found black silk
underwear in my Dad's briefcase last night," but you will also
hear words coming from these darlings' mouths that even the
editors of Playboy wouldn't publish. Likewise, you will live in a
constant state of panic over what your kid is "sharing" with the
gang when another parent is driving.

Another situation you face in carpooling is the schedule
changes. Invariably there will always be one member of the
group who is constantly jiggling the weekly driving schedule.
Her phone conversations go something like this. "I can't drive
on my Wednesday this week so I've asked Gloria to switch
with you and now you'll drive Friday, she'll drive Tuesday and
I'll take Pearl's Monday. Thursday Virginia will drive for
Gladys instead of taking the boys to Little League practice on

Saturday. That leaves you to take my Monday to drive the girls for tennis lessons. I'll pay you back a week from Wednesday when the boys have the swimming meet." Of course it should be obvious that one of two things are bound to happen here. Either all five women get in their cars to drive the carpool, or no one does. It's way too complicated for mere mortal man or woman to comprehend.

Teaching Junior the Facts of Life

Growing up in the 1950's I was a fairly ignorant specimen when it came to matters of a sexual nature. I don't recall being even remotely curious about this aspect of life until junior high school. As a student in elementary school I read all about these two kids named Dick and Jane. I read about them looking, jumping, and running after a dog named Spot. In my naiveté it never once occurred to me that when Dick and Jane grew up they would grow tired of chasing a dog all day and would find other more sordid activities to do with one another in their spare time. Not until my friends started to assemble for weekend slumber parties did I learn the gory details of what really went on with good old Dick and Jane and the rest of the world.

It's not that my parents were prudish about these things, mind you. They did all the things parents of the 50's were supposed to do. My mother bought me my first bra when I was twelve even though Bobby, the boy next door, had more under his shirt than I did. That same year she also presented me with "the book" that every young girl my age was reading behind closed bedroom doors. The cover of the book featured a single red rose and was titled, "Now That You are a Woman." Like all my friends, I was both fascinated and mildly disgusted by its contents. The book described what little surprises our bodies had in store for us during adolescence. It was informative but a little vague in certain areas, to say the least. To this day I often think about that book and am still puzzled by its cover. Call me silly but never once during my monthly reminder as a woman did I ever even think for a moment of roses, daffodils or, for that matter, any flower.

As far as any sexually explicit conversations, anything I didn't learn at the slumber parties was taught on the back of the school bus. The kids who lived the furthest from school and spent the most time on the bus were the most worldly in their knowledge of human nature. The poor kids who walked to school each day still thought the stork delivered babies until their senior year in college.

Sex education has come a long way since the "Leave it to Beaver" decade. Schools now begin teaching the basics of sexuality (a word we didn't even know in the fifties) as early as second grade and by the time your child is in her last year of elementary school she could probably tell Masters and Johnson a few things even they haven't heard yet.

Telling your child the facts of life is not nearly as difficult as knowing when and how much to tell. Many parents, myself included, make the mistake of misinterpreting a simple question their child might ask. When my son was four years old he climbed beside me on the sofa, looked into my eyes and asked the question most feared by parents everywhere, "Where did I come from?" But I was ready for this. I was one of those modern mothers who had read dozens of books on this subject. I studied countless magazine articles written by child psychologists and had purchased audio tapes on how best to respond to these delicate questions. I took three deep breaths, put my son on my lap and proceeded to tell him everything I thought his four year old mind could grasp on the subject. I started safely with the bit about the bees pollinating the flowers, moved on through every species in the animal kingdom and finally in hushed tones graphically told him about conception and birth. When I was through I lovingly looked at him and asked him if that answered his question. With that he shrugged, "Well, I guess so. Jimmy's mom just said he was from Omaha and I just got to wondering where I was from." Obviously there is a lesson to be learned here. Before you answer your child's questions, make sure you truly understand what he wants from you. I aged five years over that incident.

The fact of the matter is, if you want to be the first one to introduce your child to the facts of life, today's society has literally forced parents to do it at an earlier age than we originally intended. When I was a kid I came home from school, flipped on the T.V. and chuckled away with the "Howdy Doody Show" and "Lassie" reruns. Today a second grader comes home, grabs a Twinkie and learns about sado-masochism on the Geraldo Rivera show.

The toy industry is yet another source of sexual enlightenment for our children. Remember the good old days when the only way you knew if a doll was male or female was by the length of its hair? Except for Barbie who was born with an hourglass figure, all dolls had identical torsos. Not so anymore. Now your child can have "anatomically correct" dolls of both sexes. Girl versions come with discreetly camouflaged buttons on their backs which, when pushed, magically transform this baby doll into a hormone packed teenager complete with P.M.S. symptoms and body hair. Her male counterpart changes from adorable freckle faced Jimmy with the stubborn cowlick to Sam the college sophomore stud.

If television programs and toys haven't beaten the parents out of teaching the delicate subject of sex, then there's a pretty good chance the recording industry has. In the 1960's the

Everly Brothers recorded the hit song, "Wake Up Little Susie." The lyrics told us about this teen named Susie who was bored in a movie, fell asleep, and subsequently ruined her previously untainted reputation. Well I have news for that sixties tramp, Little Susie. By today's standard she could be Mother Superior to an order of Catholic nuns. The song lyrics our children hear today leave nothing to the imagination. Coupled with the explicit music videos on television, the kids of the nineties are more electronically sexually informed than ever before.

So whenever and however you choose to tackle this part of parenthood is ultimately your decision. Just keep in mind that if you want to be your child's first source on the subject, procrastination will be your worst enemy.

The Driving Years: Have License, Will Terrify

What I am about to discuss in the next few pages is not pretty. In fact if you are a parent of children ages ten and under you might want to spare yourself any premature stress by skipping this discussion altogether and come back to it in four or five years when the information applies. If, however, you're one of those who seeks out cheap thrills via the dark side of life, read on. Now to all you parents out there who have children with the word "teen" after their age (thirteen, fourteen, fifteen, etc.), this is definitely a must read section of the book.

As explained earlier, we know that the older a child gets, the more complicated his schedule becomes. Parents creatively shuffle their own lives around to accommodate the demands of their increasingly busy kids. Just about every parent who has spent a good portion of their lives as a chauffeur for their children has dreamed of the day when they will pass on their car keys to the next generation. Little do they know what's in store for them during the driving years.

I have a friend, Leslie, who is a classic example of what can happen to a person when their child reaches the age of driving eligibility. Leslie is just about the calmest, most collected speci-men of a mother you can find. Nothing rattles this woman. When her daughter was six years old she wanted to see if her baby brother bounced when dropped on the ceramic tile hall-way floor. Leslie heard a terrible "clunk" from the kitchen, ran to the scene of the crime and, without a moment's hesitation, proceeded to successfully administer mouth to mouth resusci-tation to the three month old infant. Never lost her cool for an instant. When she disciplines her children her voice remains a steady, sure instrument. Every challenge, dilemma and difficult situation is met with even keel determination and self compo-sure. So, when Leslie's daughter turned fifteen and was ready to begin driver's education, we figured good old Leslie would breeze through this area of parenting as efficiently as she tack-led every other facet of child rearing. Well, guess what, folks? Calm, impervious to stress, nearly comatose Leslie finally found her Achilles heel after one and a half decades of mother-ing. Sitting in the passenger seat of the family Oldsmobile while daughter Victoria burns tire rubber in the empty church parking lot, Leslie has flashbacks of herself as a child sitting on her grandfather's knee. Since grandpa's been dead over twenty-five years now, Leslie knows this probably isn't a good sign. Victoria slams on the brakes at fifty miles an hour to avoid a squirrel in the road a mere 500 yards away. With that action Leslie sees the long narrow tunnel with the bright lights that everyone who has had a near death experience talks about. When the twenty minute ordeal is over Leslie is curled up in a fetal position, blubbering in one syllable grunts and is in des-perate need of an underwear change. She crawls into the house, heads for her rosary beads and gives thanks to the Lord for sparing her life this time. She makes a solemn vow that never again will she enter the car while her daughter from Hell is behind the wheel. She throws in the towel and turns the job over to Dad, the highly decorated Air Force pilot who led

If your hair is not already "chemically dependent" on hair dyes, this is the year you'll hit the Clairol big time.

bombing raids during the Vietnam war. After a 45 minute driving session on the expressway at rush hour Dad is yelling "Mayday, Mayday!" and pulling at the buttons of his Polo shirt desperately trying to disengage the cord of his non-existent parachute. Simply put, if your hair is not already "chemically dependent" on hair dyes, this is the year you'll hit the bottle big time.

The second most frightening moment you will have as a parent of a driving age child is the day they take their actual road driving exam, leave the testing examiner's car and announce those two words which will inalterably change both yours and your child's life forever: "I passed."

Topping the list of most frightening moments, however, is the drive home from the driver's exam. Obviously there is no discussion as to which one of you gets behind the steering wheel. This is your kid's first official outing as a legitimate driver and no one is about to keep him from exercising his new right. New drivers come in two varieties. They're completely different, but both can put you into cardiac arrest. Type A is

125

the novice driver who maneuvers the city streets and freeways so slowly that even in a convertible not one hair is stirred from its place. They drive up monster inclined hills with their foot timidly on the brake pedal at all times. Eighty-five year old women with walkers strolling outside the local nursing home are faster than their cars on the street. Angry motorists blow their horns at them, shout obscenities in their direction and are forced to slam on their brakes to avoid hitting them completely. These slow drivers see so many hands thrust at them displaying the middle finger digit only, they are convinced it represents a turning symbol they neglected to learn in Driver's Ed class. The type B new driver goes so fast that his car is merely a screeching blur as it flies down the roadways of town. When this kid drives a convertible he has to keep his mouth closed or else he'd be picking mosquito parts out of his front teeth all week. Any passenger he picks up must be prepared to hop in on the run because this dude doesn't stop for anybody, anytime.

Once your child has legally acquired his driver's license, his reaction to your little helpful driving tips such as, "Ralph, I think you just ran over Mr. O'Toole's cocker spaniel," will change significantly. When he was simply a student driver in training, he would listen, although reluctantly, to your advice. Now that he is a licensed driver, suddenly he knows as much about driving as A. J. Foyt at the Indianapolis 500.

As in every area of child rearing, dealing with a child who is driving brings countless inner feelings to the surface. No other activity can even come close to the smorgasbord of emotions brought on by a child who has his or her driver's license. First there's the pride and immediate happiness you feel for your child when he waves that passing grade test paper before your eyes. Next comes the sadness when you see him drive off by himself. Although it signals a new sense of freedom for you, inwardly you can't help but feel a fresh snip at the umbilical cord which kept your child a bit closer and a bit safer with you. Next you feel the waves of anger that permeate your soul when it is one hour past curfew and your child hasn't bothered to pick up the phone to inform you of his whereabouts. Just about the time you're planning proper punishment for his delinquent ways you slowly are overpowered by a new emotion, more potent than any of the others preceding it. Fear. Cold, terror-filled fear that something bad has happened to your child. As you pace the floor and watch the clock you are literally numb with fright. You envision the worse possible scenario in your mind and find yourself making deals with the devil himself to spare your child. And then you hear the most beautiful sound a parent of a teenager can hear. The key fumbling in the door and those two glorious words, "I'm home." Relief washes over you as you run to the door, grab the kid by his shoulders and hold him close to you. With tears streaming down your face you tell him you're so happy he's back you could kill him with your bare hands.

Junior's Higher Education

One of the most often asked questions your child will encounter throughout his or her childhood is, "What do you want to be when you grow up?" If your child is like most, their response will change as often as a politician's platform during an election year. A parent can expect to hear the common career choices like astronaut, fireman, or nurse along with the not so common vocations such as magician, lion tamer or professional skateboard artist. Whatever your child decides he wants to be when asked on a Monday, the odds are pretty strong that by Wednesday of the same week his future career intentions will have taken a complete 180 degree turn.

By the time Junior is in eleventh grade, post high school plans begin to loom in his daily life. Although he might not be any further along in his future career decision than when he was in elementary school, the question "What do you want to do when you grow up?" presents a more urgent challenge than before.

Since I am writing this book from my own life experiences, I would like to cover the topic of colleges and selecting the right one both for you and your high school graduate. Let's begin with the dilemma of just how to choose a college for your child. Since I currently have two of my children in college I will use both of them as an example of how diverse this selection process can be depending on each individual kid.

Six years ago when my oldest child, Jack, was in ninth grade he visited his cousin who was a freshman at the University of Wisconsin's Madison campus. He came home from his visit, unpacked his suitcase and announced to the entire family that he, too, would be attending Madison after graduating from high school. Over the course of the next three and a half years Jack never wavered once about his decision. As quickly as college catalogues arrived in the mail, he tossed them aside without a moment's hesitation. When counselors from various universities came to his high school to promote their institutions of higher learning Jack wouldn't give them the time of day. We offered to take him on a college hunting trip just so he could be sure of his choice but our offer was turned down flatly. The subject of where our son was going to college was a closed book. He applied, was accepted, and his transition into life as a Wisconsin Badger was as uncomplicated and predictable as the change of seasons in Minnesota.

Enter child number two, a year and a half later. Our daughter Ann, like her brother, was excited and charged up over the prospect of going to college. However, to say she was a bit undecided as to where she wanted to go to further her education was a gross understatement. My husband and I were initially thrilled at her indecisiveness. Almost feeling cheated by Jack's unbudging nature a few years back, we relished the idea of experiencing the process of college selection together. We felt it would be a true bonding technique for all of us. I'm here to tell you that this little "bonding exercise" almost killed all three of us. It started safely enough. The same college brochures, pamphlets and introductory letters that Jack had thrown out two years earlier started to arrive again. I was warned by my daughter never to discard anything that came since she wanted to take every school into consideration. I bought a large manila envelope to store all the papers. Within two months the envelope became a four drawer metal filing cabinet and by summer we seriously entertained the idea of renting office space downtown to accommodate the growing collection. I finally convinced her there had to be some sort of narrowing down process to significantly reduce the choices. She agreed and after days of sifting through college leaflets she announced that she had eliminated all third world countries. It was a start. Proud of her accomplishment, it was with amazing fortitude that she continued on with the exercise and tossed aside the institutions of higher learning whose chief majors were in crop irrigation techniques and waste disposal. Her choices were now considerably narrowed to a mere 1,878 schools.

There are four words in the English language which when heard, immediately bring on dread and an overwhelming sensation of nausea. Two of these words are "teachers' strike" and the other two are "college trip." Take it from a mother who has experienced both. The latter is far worse. The scene was right out of a Norman Rockwell painting. Mother, Father, and beautiful teenage daughter snuggled lovingly in the family car ready to have the bonding experience of a lifetime. We were to visit seven colleges in five days. Sounds real warm and fuzzy, right? Well, put away your paintbrush, Norman. It ain't as easy as it looks.

Choosing which seven schools to visit was our first dilemma. We knew immediately that regardless of how clever A.A.A. was in routing road trips, the University of Hawaii and Jerusalem Tech were simply impossibilities this go around. Our trip soon began to resemble an Olympic event, a marathon of sorts which measured the number of arguments one family could have in the course of a day, how many obscenities could

**Helping your child select the right college can be a wonderful
bonding experience if it doesn't kill you in the process.**

be uttered when looking at a road map and most important
how many college sweatshirts could be purchased in a five day
time period by one eighteen year old teenager. We marveled at
the grace at which campus tour guides were able to walk back-
wards while pointing out university landmarks. We were
flooded by slick talking counselors who sang the praises of the
institutions they were representing. Ann was warned in no un-
certain terms that if she didn't choose the college they were en-
dorsing, she'd be making the mistake of a lifetime. During

these five days we visited the University of Kansas, Washington University in St. Louis, the U. of Missouri, Indiana U, Bradley University in Peoria, Illinois, Purdue and the University of Chicago. We left each school loaded down with class schedule books, pennants and massive migraines. We became irrational at one point in our quest and starting rating colleges on the quality of their fast food restaurants. Besides these seven colleges, Ann went on a school college tour and investigated Michigan, Northwestern, Iowa and our own University of Minnesota. During the entire process I had to keep reminding myself that my husband and I wanted this challenge. I couldn't help but think of Moses, the Hebrew leader who wandered for forty years in the desert. The bible said he was in search of the Promised Land. But if you want my opinion I say he was on a college search for his kid. You're probably wondering by now which school Ann finally decided on? The University of Wisconsin at Madison. Lord, give me strength.

Another major factor to consider when choosing the right college for your child is, of course, the cost. As in everything else in life different products cost different amounts. Colleges are certainly no exception. I am not about to rattle off figures about the thousands of schools in the nation and their varying tuition and housing costs. What I am going to do however is alert you to two expenditures you will encounter that no college counselor, reference manual or information packet will allude to. The first is travel expenses. When I said goodbye to Jack in the fall of 1991, I expected to see him three times during the next nine months: at Thanksgiving, winter break and spring break. He was at school for three weeks when the Minnesota Twins made it to the western league play-offs. My son is a die-hard baseball fan, and I could never forgive myself if I refused to fly him in for the games. The following week the Twins made it to the American League championship play-offs. How could I deprive my son of an experience like that?

Again we bought him an airline ticket for this once-in-a-life-time event. Two weeks later the Twins were in the World Series. Not flying Jack in for the World Series after cheering and struggling through all the play-offs was grounds for child abuse. I asked myself, "How often does a world class sporting event viewed by millions around the world come to your very own home town?" I should never have asked, for the same year the World Series took place in Minnesota was the very same year our state hosted the Superbowl, the Special Olympics, the U. S. Open and college basketball's Final Four. My son was home more that year than my friend's kid who attended the University of Minnesota. I was thrilled to have him, mind you. So was Northwest Airlines.

The second and by far and away the most costly expenditure you will have while your child is in college is your phone bill. If you don't take the situation in hand at an early stage Ma Bell will be wearing chinchilla thanks to you and to every other college parent paying their kid's phone bill. Until your son or daughter meets a new group of friends, they think nothing of picking up the phone and calling every high school buddy they ever had. And trust me when I tell you they do not bother to wait until the "peak" hours are upon them. When they get the urge to dial, there's nothing stopping them. My son has a terrific girlfriend from our home town. The only problem is that he is a year older so when he went off to college, she was still a senior in high school 300 miles away. The phone bills were staggering. Their long distance hormones were costing us a fortune. It would have been cheaper to fly her down to school each weekend except for the fact that he was already back home attending every major sporting event known to mankind. Tuition was manageable, housing was a stretch, but the price tag on the phone bills were putting us into bankruptcy. Somehow we survived the year and blessed the day when Jack's girlfriend received her acceptance letter to the University of Wisconsin the following year. After the experience with our son we put forth new stricter guidelines in regard to our daughter Ann and any future boyfriends. We didn't care if they drank like a fish, smoked illegal substances or were convicted felons. As long as they went to the same college that she did, it was OK with us.

Epilogue

Regardless of what stage of parenting you are currently enrolled in, be it the baking stage (better known as pregnancy) or the master's level (college age) it is crucial to maintain a healthy sense of humor at all times. There will be countless situations when new parents will ask themselves, "What did we get ourselves into?" When these moments arise the wisest thing to do is to somehow struggle along during the day, try if possible to see the funny side of the dilemma and then reassess the situation when your child is asleep that evening. For any parent who has ever watched a son or daughter peacefully slumber amidst an army of stuffed bears and dinosaurs will somehow forget the root beer stain on the sofa, the crayon smudges on the wallpaper and the broken china vase in the den. What they see instead are only dreams and hopes for their child's future. They replay the day's events over and over in their minds as they watch this sleeping child. They remember the happiness, frustration, fear, anger, intolerance, and helplessness they felt. And as they lean over quietly to kiss this baffling creature goodnight they know that sitting high above all the other emotions they might have felt during this challenging day is the strongest and mightiest of them all:

Love.